SCOTTISH MILITARY DRESS

SCOTTISH MILITARY DRESS

PETER COCHRANE

illustrated by Jeffrey Burn

BLANDFORD PRESS
LONDON · NEW YORK · SYDNEY

First published in the UK 1987 by Blandford Press
Link House, West Street, Poole, Dorset BH15 1LL

Copyright © 1987 Peter Cochrane

Distributed in the United States by
Sterling Publishing Co, Inc,
2 Park Avenue, New York, NY 10016

Distributed in Australia by
Capricorn Link (Australia) Pty Ltd
PO Box 665, Lane Cove, NSW 2066

British Library Cataloguing in Publication Data

Cochrane, Peter
  Scottish military dress. — (Uniforms
  and history).
  1. Great Britain. *Army. Scottish regiments*
  — Uniforms — History   2. Scotland
  — History, Military
  I. Title   II. Burn, Jeffrey   III. Series
  355.1'4'09411   UC485.G7

ISBN 0 7137 1738 6

Typeset and printed in Great Britain by
Butler & Tanner Ltd, Frome, Somerset

CONTENTS

INTRODUCTION

This is a short book on a large subject. As such it can do no more than present a selection of the many forms, and variations within forms, of Scottish military dress from the seventeenth century until today, although I hope that the twin threads of continuity and change will be apparent. There is a reason for every change in dress and equipment, and to set these reasons in context I have included brief notes on the historical background where it is relevant, and on the circumstances in which Scottish regiments were raised.

It does not claim however to be a series of regimental histories, still less a history of tartan and Highland dress, largely as they must feature in an account like this; some books in both fields are listed in the Bibliography.

There have been many changes in the numbering and in the titles of Scottish, and particularly Highland regiments, which can be confusing. The changes are summarised in the Appendix, with the exclusion of units disbanded before 1881. In the captions to the colour plates, I have for simplicity used the pre-1881 regimental number, despite the fact that this is an anachronism in the seventeenth century.

My debt to previous writers in this field, and to regimental historians, is great; I must single out Lieutenant-Colonel Angus Fairrie's *Cuidich 'n Righ: A History of the Queen's Own Highlanders (Seaforth and Camerons)* as an example of a history which also describes dress in detail. I am grateful to the National Library of Scotland and to the National Portrait Gallery of Scotland, and would like to express particular thanks to Mr W. G. F. Boag of the Scottish United Services Museum in Edinburgh Castle, and to its invaluable library. It would be presumptuous, perhaps, to hope that there are no errors in this little book; any that exist are mine.

I: LATE MIDDLE AGES

Historians today demur at the foreshortened view of early Scotland as a country suffering from almost uninterrupted warfare—between neighbours, when there was no outside enemy to fight against. It remains true however that external and internal pressures produced societies in the Lowlands and the Highlands in which a summons to take up arms was far from rare. Fighting was not a way of life but to some degree a part of life, and for most people therefore it did not call for special clothes; you answered the summons with your weapon, wearing the clothes in which you went to work.

Military dress existed only among those wealthy enough to buy armour of one kind or another, a small number in a poor country. But Scotland traded actively with all the countries round the North Sea, from Norway to France, in addition to its links with England, and armour came from a number of sources to supplement what Scottish smiths could make. There were fashions in armour, as in anything else, and it appears that Scotland was a century or so behind the Continent, as it was in architecture. Some forms of armour of course, such as full plate, could never have figured largely in Scotland because the country did not breed the heavy horses needed to carry its weight.

West Highland grave slabs show a characteristic recumbent warrior wearing a high-pointed bascinet or helmet and a mail 'chest protector' which also covered the throat and in some cases seems to cover the head under the helmet. The body was protected by a gambeson of heavy padded material which fell below the knee and could be worn over a mail shirt. It is not clear whether there was any protection for the legs. A long, two-handed sword, the claymore, is held by a waistbelt—a weapon of great antiquity, for Tacitus describes the 'huge' and 'enormous' swords of the Britons of Caledonia, adding that they were unmanageable in close-quarter fighting against the Romans.

Some slabs show the warrior carrying a spear, with a 'heater'-type of shield on the left arm. Figure A, based upon one of these at Iona, shows a variation in that the padded gambeson has given way to a surcoat worn over mail, with apparently some armour, or possibly mail, for the legs and feet. This resembles armour worn in England in the thirteenth century, but the Iona slab is probably at least a century more recent. One grave there, which can be dated as no older

9

Figure 1

than 1519, still shows this general style. The stone carvers clearly used a stereotyped figure, so in addition to the problem of dating, the details of the armour are unreliable; a standardised effigy of a warrior may have marked the grave of any local man of distinction who was not a priest, whether or not he had owned or worn armour.

The same difficulty occurs with seals. Robert Bruce's Great Seal shows a mailed warrior, wearing a flat-topped war helm and brandishing a short, heavy sword, at full gallop on his splendidly caparisoned horse. But the same design, albeit with a different heraldic charge on the shield, appears elsewhere. We are looking at an image, not a representation.

We lack even the unsatisfactory evidence of grave slabs to tell us what was worn by the levies in daily life and in the wars. There were two kinds of military service upon which the king could call. 'Free service' was owned by freeholders, a category which included the nobility who could be expected to possess some armour and to be mounted, while 'Scottish service' or 'Scottish army' consisted of the peasantry, armed as a rule with spear or axe. The former, a feudal service, proved of little value against heavy horse; the Wars of Independence were won by 'Scottish service' which had its roots in an earlier, wholly Celtic Scotland.

Highlanders and Islesmen formed part of Bruce's army at Bannockburn, but by the end of the Middle Ages a clear distinction had emerged between the Lowlands and the still Celtic, Gaelic-speaking Highlands, even if the boundary between the two was fuzzy. Because it looked so strange to southerners, early Highland dress was described by a number of travellers whose observations are of varying reliability. Its singularity lay both in the material and in the garment it formed.

The early Scots may have brought with them from Ireland the *leine chroich*, an outer garment of linen, perhaps padded or quilted, which was dyed saffron when worn by notables; but it was the striped or variegated mantle which caught the eye of sixteenth-century observers. The derivation of the word 'tartan' is obscure, perhaps connected with the French *tiretaine*, a type of fine cloth, perhaps with the Erse *tuar*, colour. It has always been used with both connotations, no doubt because from a very early date the thin, hard cloth of the Highlands was woven from dyed yarn in patterns of squares or checks, the easiest way of weaving a decorative cloth.

Tartan is by tradition a twill weave i.e. two weft threads pass under two, then over two warp threads, the latter being staggered to give the twill its diagonal effect. The pattern (the number of pairs of threads in each colour) is the same both up and down and across, and thus, to quote James Scarlett, 'an area of solid colour can only be bounded by an area of mixed colour'. Hence, too, the apparent number of colours in a tartan: 'a tartan that starts off with four basic colours will finish up with ten colours or mixtures'. The sett in tartan means the proportion of threads of a given colour to those of another colour. Since the exact colours can vary, the sett is the only accurate description.

Colour variation in actual tartan, as distinct from the limitations of colour printing, is due to the dyes that have been used and to the process of dyeing. In the days of hand dyeing small quantities at a time, with vegetable dyes extracted from local plants, the variation was very marked. Age and use also change the appearance of, and the balance between, different colours; even with twentieth-century dyes, the same sett woven in 1915, 1930 and 1940, after hard wear, can look at first glance like different tartans.

Two lengths of tartan were sewn together to form a rectangle about five feet wide and fifteen or eighteen feet long to make a plaid (Gaelic *plaide* or blanket). It was worn in the Lowlands as a cloak, often with a pattern of simple checks, and in the Highlands as the *breacan feileadh* or belted plaid, in a much richer range of pattern and colour (*breacan* means mottled or variegated and *feileadh* is a fold or pleat). Woven from tightly twisted yarn, the cloth was much more waterproof than modern tartan cloth.

The belted plaid had the great advantage of needing no tailoring to meet its function as a combined upper and nether garment which was also a blanket at night. Its disadvantage would seem to be that, to put it on, the wearer had to spread it on the ground (which in Scotland can be wet). For an accurate opinion I am indebted to Jeffrey Burn, the illustrator of this book, who owns and wears a full-size belted plaid. He says the process of putting it on is simple and quick, as shown in the illustration opposite.

When the belted plaid was put on, the pleating was not confined to the back of the lower part as in the later kilt; illustrations of this period often show one or more broad pleats at the front also. Because the *breacan feileadh* or *feileadh mhor* was the usual dress of the Highlands, it was the dress of the fighting man and continued to be so into the eighteenth century. As an alternative, *triubhas*, or trews, might be worn, often with a separate plaid, by the upper rank of Highlander; these too were of tartan cloth, but cut on the bias to give a close fit on the leg. With both belted plaid and trews, the gentry came to wear a short jacket, also of tartan.

But what tartan? Highland garb and its essential feature, tartan, suffered in the nineteenth century from much romanticised and spurious history, and it was claimed that every clan from time immemorial had worn its own distinctive tartan. This is now recognised as mythology. Instead it is thought that different areas of the Highlands may well have developed a tradition of weaving certain setts in colours which would at least partly reflect the local availability of dyestuffs. A group of related setts would thus be predominantly reddish in background, or dark green, etc.

Unlike the later kilt (see p. 32), the belted plaid could be adjusted to have more or less of its length above and below the waist. As late as 1725–26, when he wrote his *Letters from a Gentleman in the North of Scotland*, Edward Burt commented that 'for the most part they wear the Petticoat so very short, that on a windy Day, going up a Hill, or stooping, the Indecency of it is plainly

01382   3544

discovered'. He also observed that Highlanders were fond of punctuating a conversation with a fling of their plaid over the shoulder, a gesture which released a disagreeable smell from the garment worn all day and sweated in at night. We too must avoid the danger of romanticising.

1640's.

TARTAN LENGTH

MIDDLE SECTION ROUGHLY PLEATED WITH A BELT UNDERNEATH. THE MAN LIES DOWN WITH THE BOTTOM LEVEL JUST ABOVE HIS KNEES. HE WRAPS EACH SIDE OVER HIM AND DOES UP THE BELT, AND THEN STANDS UP.

AS HE STANDS UP THE LARGE LOOSE AREA FALLS DOWN LOOKING MOST UNSIGHTLY.

THE LOOSE PART IS TWISTED AND PULLED OVER THE SHOULDER AND TUCKED OR TIED UNDERNEATH THE WAIST BELT THE SIDE FLAPS ARE TUCKED INTO THEMSELVES TO MAKE POCKETS.

THE LATER BELTED-PLAID DIFFERS ONLY IN THE ATTACHMENT TO THE SHOULDER WITH A BROOCH.

Figure 2

13

II: SEVENTEENTH CENTURY

Since there was no standing army before the Restoration in 1660, there were no professional soldiers employed in Scotland although there were plenty of Scots serving in foreign armies, above all the Swedish and the Dutch. Gustavus Adolphus of Sweden is said to have had ten thousand Scots in his service, a suspect number; but it is certain that in 1632 there were more than one hundred Scotsmen who held Swedish commissions in addition to 'diverse Captaines and Inferiour Officers'. Their collective experience, embodied in Alexander Leslie, a field marshal of Sweden, was invaluable when the Estates of Scotland decided to defy Charles I and called out the long-disused national army, putting it under Leslie's command.

This was the 'Scottish service' mentioned early in Chapter I. All able-bodied men between the ages of sixteen and sixty were liable to serve for a period usually limited to forty days. For poorer subjects, there was sometimes the concession that they would not be ordered to cross the Border.

Uniform in this army was non-existent except for the fact that in the Lowlands the universal dress was a coat and breeches of undyed country cloth or homespun, the famous 'hodden grey'. In Highlands and Lowlands alike the head-dress was a flat bonnet, usually dark blue. Clearly clothing had to be supplied to these levies, for the responsible committee of the Estates in 1640 'took exact tryell what gray claith ... the marchandis had' and despatched to the army twenty thousand 'suits and socks'. They did wear a distinguishing badge, however. Spalding records that 'few or none of this haill army wantit ane blew ribbin hung about his crag down under his left arme, quilk they call it *the covenanteris ribbin*', while Patrick Gordon calls the Scots army in Northumberland in 1640 'the blew ribbons and blew cappes' (both quoted by Terry). The blue scarf does not seem to have been worn in later campaigns in the Civil Wars.

The King backed away from battle in 1639, and in 1640 Leslie's troops invaded England, occupying Newcastle and halting the coal trade. Charles was forced to negotiate an agreement, and after terms had been settled, Leslie paraded his army, presumably as a warning that the agreement must be honoured. The English observers were particularly struck by the presence of Highlanders among the Covenanters' forces: 'commonly called Redshanks, with their plaides cast over their shoulders, having every one his bowe and arrowes with a broad slycing sword by his side' (Figure 1).

Plate 1
Figure 1

The claymore had fallen into disuse, not doubt because its length and the need to use two hands to wield it made it too cumbersome a weapon, and had been replaced by the broadsword. The bow for long remained a much better weapon than the musket, in terms of accuracy, penetration and, above all, rate of fire—the matchlock musketeer might get off a round every two minutes. But to be effective the bow had to be handled by a trained man, whose training had started in youth, whereas it was comparatively easy to train a musketeer. A large body of them, firing in sequence, could compensate for the musket's notorious inaccuracy and slow rate of fire. In earlier days it had been the bowmen of the Selkirk Forest who provided archers for the army, but the bow was by now restricted to the Highlands. In 1644, Alasdair MacColla or MacDonald ('Colkitto') brought one thousand men from Antrim and the Isles to join Montrose; they were armed with muskets, while most of Montrose's Highlanders were bowmen. By the 1680s, the musket had replaced the bow.

The belted plaid was worn over a long shirt which according to an eighteenth-century source was sometimes daubed with pitch, no doubt as a form of weather-proofing. Montrose's victory at Kilsyth in August 1645 was on a day so hot that his men threw off their plaids and fought in their shirts, with the long tails tied between their legs. We can assume that the shirts were more or less white because Montrose ordered his cavalry to wear a white shirt over their other clothes, to give some sort of uniform appearance to his little army.

Hose were worn with the belted plaid; they were not knitted but made from cloth, often patterned, and like the trews were cut on the bias to give a tighter fit. Frequently however the Highlanders went bare-legged in their *cuaran* or deer-hide shoes—hence the nickname of 'redshanks'.

One of the reasons for Montrose's brilliant if short-lived success was the fact that the bulk of the Scottish army was in England. Under the Solemn League and Covenant, the Estates were allied with the English Parliament in the Civil War, and in August 1643 had ordered out 'fencible persons of all ranks and degrees'. They had to provide themselves with forty days' provisions, and weapons. Horsemen were to bring pistols, broadswords and steel caps or, failing them, 'jackes or secreites, lances and steil bonnettes'. One of them is illustrated in Figure 2.

Plate 1
Figure 2

There are records of Scottish cavalry charging on the battlefield, but their normal role was scouting, skirmishing and breaking up small bodies of enemy footmen, since their mounts were not heavy enough for shock tactics. Horsemen came in the main from the north-east, which tended to be royalist and episcopalian in sentiment, and from the Borders which had a long tradition of mounted raiders, lightly armed and capable of swift movement across difficult country—the reivers of the ballads. The greater part of the Covenanters' cavalry were Borderers, in many cases no doubt wearing their father's or grandfather's 'steil bonnette', for the area had still been turbulent a generation earlier. The jack or buffil coat was of leather, short-sleeved and laced across the chest. A 'secreite' was defensive armour worn under an outer coat, and could also refer to a metal skull-cap worn under a bonnet or a hat. The lance was a lighter version of the footman's pike.

One is inclined to think of the Covenanting army as a somewhat sombre body of men, and indeed the clothing of the rank and file was more sober, and more practical, than uniforms were to be for two hundred and fifty years. Yet, as **Plate 2 Figure 3** shows, the case was different for officers of at least some regiments. Captain Keith of the Mearns and Aberdeen Regiment received a mercer's bill in May 1644 for 'mixt Spanish cloth' for breeches; 'scarlet cloth and satin ribbon' for his coat and lining; '4½ disane gold and silver long-tail'd buttons; pearle cullor silk stockings; buckskin gloves, 2 Demibaver hatts and two bands' (beaver or felt hats). The silk stockings would have been worn under woollen ones in the field. The account totalled £15 5s. which represented two months pay for a captain, and Keith still had to meet the tailor's bill for making up the material—and for sewing on the fifty-four buttons, which perhaps decorated his sleeves as well as forming a long row down the front of his almost knee-length coat. He would certainly have been conspicuous amongst his men in their hodden grey.

When 'fencible persons of all ranks and degrees' had been called out, footmen had to provide themselves, in addition to provisions, with a musket or a pike; in lieu of that a sword and a halberd, a Lochaber axe or a Jedburgh stave. The last was a pole with a long, very narrow blade fixed to its top two feet, while a Lochaber axe was a combined spear and axe. There must have been some recalcitrance in obeying the ordinance, for eighteen months later it was enacted that a man mustering without a musket who had the means to buy one would be fined £1 13s. 4d. (20 pounds Scots) or 10 merks if in the same circumstances he turned up without a pike. If 'nather yeoman nor servant' could afford it, the 'maister or heritour' had to provide the means. A musket cost 15s., a pair of pistols for a horseman, 40s.

The foot soldier in Figure 4 wears the blue scarf which the Covenanting army **Plate 2 Figure 4** of 1639–40 displayed. As a pikeman, he was superior to a musketeer. The pike was still an essential weapon for the infantry of all armies, and was particularly dear to the Scots. At Bannockburn it was the schiltroms, solid phalanxes of spearmen, which proved impregnable to the English heavy cavalry and, when they moved forward in the offensive, ground through horse and foot, although sixteen years earlier at Falkirk, Wallace's schiltroms had been destroyed where they stood by devastating English archery. In the seventeenth century, the pikemen's tasks were to protect musketeers during the slow process of reloading and, in the advance, to drive off enemy infantry by 'push of pike'.

His weapon was fifteen to eighteen feet long, a narrow-bladed iron spearhead rivetted to an ash shaft (the half-pike carried by officers later in the century was nine feet long). In the 1640s, the Scottish army had two pikemen for every three musketeers, a proportion which later dwindled in all armies with the introduction of the bayonet and the gradual supersession of the matchlock musket by the less inefficient flintlock. Marlborough decided that pikemen were a waste of potential fire-power, and pikes disappeared from the army in 1706.

The belted plaid was an unsuitable garment for riding, another reason for chiefs and leaders to wear the trews. Montrose is recorded on several occasions as 'cled in cot and trewis as the Irishes was cled', Irishes meaning both his Highland followers and the MacDonnells of Antrim. Figure 5 shows one of his officers so dressed, without the plaid which could be worn as a cloak. Later illustrations of this dress show coat, trews and plaid of different tartans, which was probably also the case in the seventeenth century.

Plate 2
Figure 5

Since the tartan did not differentiate one body of Highlanders from another, a distinguishing badge was sometimes worn in the shape of a sprig of some plant, as in this picture. In the nineteenth century, every clan had its own badge ascribed to it, rowan for instance, or bog-myrtle, but these may be as suspect as the clan tartans invented in the same period. There is no doubt that all seventeenth-century armies had a problem in identification of their own and enemy troops, and that for a set-piece battle men would be ordered to wear a badge in their hats; a scrap of white paper or a wisp of hay are both mentioned. At the same time the rallying-cry for the day would be issued, which ranged from the obvious, such as *Victory!*, to the Covenanters' gruesome *Jesus and No Quarter!* at Philiphaugh where the remnants of Montrose's forces were put to the sword in 1645.

Relations between the partners in the Solemn League and Covenant deteriorated. In 1648, after Charles I, a prisoner in the Isle of Wight, had secretly engaged to support presbyterianism in Scotland, the Scots demanded that he should be released and marched an army into England, to be defeated by Cromwell at Preston. There was no force left to halt the trial and execution of the king, an event which led at once to the proclamation in Scotland of Charles II, who had signed the Covenants, no doubt with tongue in cheek. The royal cause was not accepted by the extreme Covenanters and even less so by the army which governed England. Cromwell crossed the Border in July 1650 to confront an army similar to that raised by the Estates in 1639 and, like it, commanded by Leslie, now Earl of Leven, although the actual commander was his namesake David Leslie. His skilful manoeuvring forced Cromwell into a bad position at Dunbar, where the Scots threw away their advantage and suffered a crushing defeat.

Yet another army was hastily raised by the royalists and moderate presbyterians. Charles II was crowned at Scone in January 1651, and when Cromwell advanced on Perth later that year, leaving open the way into England, Charles led his army south. He found no recruits, and Cromwell had little difficulty in wiping out the invaders at Worcester, his third rout of a Scots army in four years.

With Charles II's Restoration in 1660, we can trace the foundation of a regular standing army in Scotland and in England, and with it the beginnings of an unbroken sequence in the history of military dress. A standing army was a distrusted institution in both countries. In some quarters this was due to fears of royal power, with the example of Louis XIV across the Channel, but in Scotland there was additionally resentment at nine years of military occupation by the Cromwellian army—years, in fact, of good government but of heavy taxation to pay for the occupying forces. Although the Scottish Estates passed a Militia Act in 1663 providing for the raising in an emergency of twenty thousand foot and two thousand horse for the king's service in Scotland, England and Ireland, regular forces were another matter. Funds were grudgingly voted, on what was to become an annual basis, by the two Parliaments and, after the Union of 1707, by the new Parliament of Great Britain. More money was forthcoming when war was imminent but the regiments raised as a result usually had to be disbanded when the crisis was over.

Until the Union, Scotland had its own military establishment, as Ireland continued to do, but it is scarcely true to say that Scotland still maintained its own army. Regiments were carried on the Scottish or Irish establishments to spread the cost of the king's army over the countries that produced the tax revenue. Ironically, the senior Scottish regiment, and the oldest regiment in the British army, now known as the Royal Scots, was borne on the English establishment. It dates its foundation to a charter given by Charles I in 1633 to Sir John Hepburn to raise recruits in Scotland for service on the Continent. Hepburn had previously soldiered with a Scots company in Bohemia and Holland, had expanded it into a regiment in the Swedish army under Gustavus Adolphus, and now combined those veterans with his new recruits into *le Régiment d'Hebron* in the service of Louis XIII of France. Hepburn was created a *Maréchal de France* and killed in action in 1636, command passing to Lord George Douglas who became Earl of Dumbarton in 1675. The regiment was accordingly known as Douglas's and then Dumbarton's, although in 1666 it is called the Scotch Regiment of Foot in the *London Gazette*. It came to England at the Restoration but again returned to the service of France where it remained—apart from a brief return to England during the Second Dutch War—until its final recall in 1678.

Charles II acquired Tangier as part of the dowry of his Portuguese bride, and the 'First of Foot' served in its garrison from 1680 to 1683 with sufficient distinction to earn its title of the Royal Regiment of Foot in 1684. A painting of the regiment there, attributed to Dirck Stoop, is in the National Maritime Museum at Greenwich. A detail shows, rather indistinctly, four pipers standing on a knoll, playing while the soldiers labour at the demolition of the mole

Plate 3
Figure 6
(Tangier had proved a costly liability and was abandoned to the Moors). It is on this that Figure 6 is based.

The pipers wear the same uniform as the rank and file, which consisted of a long red coat, grey breeches and grey stockings. The head-dress was a low-crowned black hat, the brim of which appears to be slightly turned up all round. They carry no sword, but would undoubtedly have been equipped with some side-arm, if only a knife. Our piper is shown 'blowing up' the bag before starting to play; note that his pipes have only two drones instead of the later three. These pipers were carried on the books, and paid, as 'centinels' or private men, although one piper was officially carried; in 1689, there is a reference to the 'piper to the colonel's company' and in a 1705 list of rates of pay for regiments of foot there occurs the entry 'Piper (Royal Regt. only)'. His pay was 1s. a day in contrast to the 8d. listed for 'grenadiers, privates, sentinels and fusiliers'.

A list published by Nathan White in 1684 gives the dress of an officer of the Royal Regiment as a red coat lined with white; white sash with a white fringe; Plate 3
Figure 7 and light grey breeches and stockings, as depicted in Figure 7. When the coat was left open, or turned back at the collar or cuffs, the lining was visible in a contrasting colour to the coat. The material on lapels, collar and cuffs came to be called facings as distinct from the lining, but at this time and into the eighteenth century facings and lining were synonymous, and therefore the same colour. In Flanders in 1692, the regiment still had white linings to their coats, and not blue, which became the distinction of royal regiments. Some Scots units changed the colour of their linings when the Scottish establishment was merged with the English after the Union in 1707, but, as was noted above, the Royals had always been on the English establishment.

There exists a Treasury Warrant of 1687 to the Customs authorising the export, duty free, from England to Scotland of a cargo of goods shipped by the Earl of Dumbarton. It included '500 felt hats for serjeants and soldiers; 500 pairs of worsted hose for corporals and soldiers; 207 pairs of worsted hose for officers, serjeants and drummers; ... scarlet and blue cloth for officers: pieces of shalloon for lining.' This could be taken as indicating a change in facings or linings for officers, but it is hard to square with the apparent continuance of white linings in 1692.

The black felt hat was to be worn almost throughout the army for more than another century, contorted into various shapes despite the fact that in its original, basic form the brim must have kept the sun out of the eyes and stopped rain getting down the neck. Officers' hats at this period were often adorned with a large feather, though it is not clear whether the style and colour were the choice of the colonel or of the individual officer. One side of the brim was pinned up and this seems to have been the rule for all ranks in many regiments by the end of the century.

Plate 3
Figure 8 A musketeer of about the same date, 1689, is shown in Figure 8. His regiment was raised in that year by David Melville, 3rd Earl of Leven (see below, p. 23),

and later became the King's Own Scottish Borderers. His dress is standard for the time—red coat with a white neck-cloth, grey breeches and stockings, brass buckles to his shoes and the usual black felt hat. A musketeer had to have some weapon in addition to his firing piece, and for long this had been a sword. The bayonet was a new piece of equipment, and a very unsatisfactory one since it was plugged into the muzzle of the musket; it not only put the musket out of action but was likely to split the muzzle. For some time, as in this picture, a sword was carried as well as the plug-bayonet, on the 'belt and braces' principle.

His musket is the old matchlock, as can be seen from the fact that he carries a bandolier with its dangling charges, the so-called Twelve Apostles. After ramming home the load, the musketeer had to place the correct quantity of fine powder in the priming pan which could then be ignited by the match—a smouldering length of specially prepared cord.

Various dates are put forward for the founding of the regiment now known as the Scots Guards, but since the 'Lifeguard of Foot' formed by Charles II in 1650 suffered heavily at Dunbar and was annihilated at Worcester, it is safe to plump for 1662 when the restored king signed a warrant for 'a New Regiment of Foot Guards to his Majestie consisting of 600 Souldiers'. It too had pipers on the strength, as private men; it is an error to think of the pipes as a peculiarly Highland instrument, or that pipes were unknown in the army until the raising of the first Highland regiment two generations later. It is interesting that the regiment's muster roll of 1676 identifies pipers, and that their names are Lowland, such as Miller and Morton.

In 1679, the regiment was in action at Bothwell Brig where a Covenanting insurrection was defeated. There are two paintings, by de Witt and Jan Wyck,

Plate 4
Figure 9

of two different stages in the battle; Figure 9 is based on the former. It shows a sergeant, carrying a halberd as the sign of his rank. He wears a red coat with a white lining which shows as a facing down the front, but the turn-ups to his cuffs are red, without any facing. A white undercoat is visible; this had long sleeves and was the forerunner of the long-sleeved waistcoat which was for long to remain a feature of military dress. The painter has given officers and sergeants a white plume in their black hat, and has depicted all ranks in very dark grey breeches and stockings. Jan Wyck in addition shows some pikemen, wearing grey coats and red stockings and perhaps red breeches. This appears to be an example of the English custom of dressing pikemen in reversed colours to musketeers, but one cannot be certain of their regiment.

In 1686, the year after Charles II's death and the accession of James VII and II, the Scottish Regiment of Foot Guards was amongst the regiments in the 'List of King James's Army on Hounslow Heath', no longer wearing grey breeches

Plate 4
Figure 10

and stockings but white (Figure 10). The red coat and white undercoat were unchanged, but the men's hats were now ornamented as sergeants' had been, with white tape round the edge of the brim, and a white ribbon round the low crown. Musketeers in all regiments were beginning to be armed with flintlock muskets instead of matchlocks, and for Guards regiments the process was complete by this date. The change-over took much longer for infantry of the Line, and it has been estimated that by the end of the century half the musketeers in some regiments were still equipped with matchlocks. The flintlock was no more accurate than its predecessor, but it obviated the need for a slow match, with its twin perils of being extinguished in heavy rain or of igniting much more than the powder in the priming-pan. The introduction of made-up cartridges, carried in a 'cartouche-box' fixed to the waistbelt, made the bandolier redundant.

The danger of a continuously burning match was most acute when carried by the soldiers protecting an artillery train with its tubs of powder open during action, and they were among the first to be equipped with a form of flintlock, slightly lighter than the standard flintlock musket, and known as a fusil. The fusiliers armed with them carried out a normal infantry role, and were not restricted to guarding the gunners. The regiment known much later as the Royal Scots Fusiliers was raised in 1678 under a commission granted to the Earl of Mar and seems to have embodied an independent company previously commanded by him. They were armed at the outset like other infantry with matchlocks. It is probable that their uniform was a grey coat and breeches, but in the 1680s the coat was red while the breeches remained grey. Their nickname was the Earl of Mar's Greybreeks, which is odd in view of the fact that all Scottish troops of the time wore breeches of that colour. John Buchan, the regiment's historian, suggests that 'greybreeks' was the generic term for a soldier in Scotland as 'redcoat' was in England, but this is hardly likely since hodden grey was the countryman's usual garb in the Lowlands.

Plate 5
Figure 11
The drummer in Figure 11 is based on a description given by Buchan. Drummers were always very distinctively uniformed because of their function in battle. The beat of drum transmitted orders for tactical movement in the face of the enemy, when cohesion was much more important than on parade or on the line of march. A mystique attached to the drums themselves, and almost as much disgrace was incurred by a regiment's loss of its drums to the enemy as the loss of its colours.

Reversed colours in one form or another was a popular distinction for a drummer's uniform, and in this case his 'purple' (i.e. plum-coloured) coat and red breeches are a ground for thinking that the regiment's dress at this time consisted of grey coat and breeches.

Plate 5
Figure 12
The 'Greybreeks' also had pipers (Figure 12), dressed like the rank and file as were the pipers in the Tangier garrison. The regimental rolls list three pipers in 1682 as 'sentinells'. It was only a few years later that the uniform changed to a red coat and a new style of head-dress when Mar's Regiment became 'Fuzileers' about 1685.

A grenadier company had already been added to the regiment, following the example of the Guards who were the first Scots unit to take this step. Grenadiers were the assault force of a regiment and therefore men picked for their height. Unlike those of the rest of the battalion, their muskets were fitted with slings, to leave both arms free when they threw their grenades; and because a slung musket caught the brim of the usual felt hat, grenadiers wore a special cap. In a fusilier regiment, which also had slings on its muskets, the whole battalion wore this **Plate 5** cap. As will be seen in Figure 13 which shows an officer of the regiment, the **Figure 13** grenadier cap began life as a much simpler item of dress than it was to develop into.

The bag-cap was one of the earliest forms of working head-dress, still to be seen in eighteenth-century pictures of sailors or millers, for example, and surviving long after then as a night-cap. It was an elementary first step for the purpose of military identification to fix a plate or panel to the brim, carrying a badge of some description. At this date the bag of the cap hung down, but very soon a stiffened front was added, to the top of which the bag was attached to give a smarter appearance. It was made taller to add to the soldier's height, an increasingly important aspect of military head-dress, and the front plate was later enlarged also.

This officer's dress displays a feature unique to the regiment until it became a royal one—the red coat is lined and faced in the same colour, and under it was worn a red waistcoat. The half-pike he carries was a usual sign of commissioned rank until in 1710 Marlborough ordered officers to carry the somewhat shorter (seven foot) 'espontoon' or spontoon.

Another famous regiment raised in the reign of Charles II is known to history as the Scots Greys. Two companies of horse, raised in 1678, were strengthened with additional troops in 1681 to become the Royal (Scots) Dragoons, which thus started life as a royal regiment. Its first colonel was the formidable Thomas Dalziell who had been taken prisoner at Worcester, escaped and fought for the Emperor of Russia until the Restoration. He was given leave to import from England 2,436 ells of stone-grey cloth for the new regiment, and in 1684, when the Privy Council in Scotland licensed officers to import cloth for their men with the stipulation that 'all the cloth imported for the soldiers to be red or scarlet', Dalziell was again permitted to import 100 ells of grey cloth for his officers and 1,100 ells for his men. It was almost certainly from their clothing and not from their horses that the regiment was commonly known as the Grey Dragoons. **Plate 6** Figure 14 shows an officer of this period in his workman-like uniform, the only **Figure 14** touch of colour being his red sash.

Dragoons were not categorised as horse. They were in effect mounted infantry who fought on foot once they had ridden to the point of action; one man in ten had then to act as a horse-holder. Long, stiff cavalry boots would have made dismounted movement difficult, and so the riding boots of dragoons were made from pliable leather.

Plate 6
Figure 15

Dalziell died in 1685. Within two years his regiment was wearing red coats. A note dated 1687 amongst the regimental papers in the Scottish United Services Museum states that the cost of a private's coat is £1 18s. 4d. and specifies 5½ ells of red cloth, and 6 ells of blue serge for the lining, with 'tin buttons'. Breeches are not mentioned, and it is presumed that they remained grey until some time before 1707, when they were certainly blue. Figure 15 is a soldier of the grenadier troop in the 1687 uniform. In that year the dragoon's weapons were recorded as a snaphance (or fusil) with barrels three feet eight inches long and carried on a sling across the body, a bayonet and a hatchet.

There is controversy over their head-dress. One account has it that the whole regiment was granted the distinction, unique amongst dragoons, of wearing a grenadier cap in recognition of their feat at the battle of Ramillies in 1706 of capturing an entire French regiment. Other authorities point out that the cap was worn much earlier than 1706, but only by the grenadier troop. From the regimental papers it seems that in 1692 they had two head-dresses since a supply of 333 'dragoons' caps' is mentioned, and it also appears that the hats had harder wear than the caps, for the men had a new hat annually, a new cap every two years. These dragoons' caps may have been forage caps, and nothing to do with grenadier caps.

James's short reign was marked in Scotland by measures of stern represssion, carried out by the military, against the strict Covenanters or 'conventiclers'. Whether the army relished the task is not clear, but it is certain that, like the army in England, they were alarmed by James's action in removing Protestant officers in the regiments in Ireland and replacing them with Roman Catholics. In 1688, most of the regular forces in Scotland had been moved south to counter the expected invasion from Holland, but when William of Orange landed only a handful of officers was prepared to maintain their allegiance to the discredited James. In Scotland, however, the Stewart adherents were still a force to be taken into account, a fact which led to the raising of two new regiments.

The Estates were summoned to meet in Edinburgh in March 1689, where the 'Williamites' prevailed over the 'Jacobites' although the Duke of Gordon held the Castle for James and posed a threat to the Parliament House. The Earl of Leven, commissioned to form a regiment, raised eight hundred men, in two hours it is said: see page 19. He paraded his recruits at St Giles's to protect the Estates, which a month later denounced the 'levying or keeping on foot a standing army in time of peace'; it depended, of course, on whose army was in question. Leven's corps was thus so closely linked with the city that it became known as the Edinburgh Regiment.

It was in action four months later as part of the force assembled under General Mackay to crush a Jacobite rising led by James Graham of Claverhouse, Earl of Dundee. Dundee had acquired a sinister reputation, to some extent undeserved, as a ruthless oppressor of the 'conventiclers'; he now showed himself to be an able tactician and an inspired leader of his Highlanders. He faced Mackay at Killiecrankie and, in perhaps the best-known example of the famous Highland charge, destroyed the 'Williamites' in ten minutes of close-quarter fighting in which the Highland broadswords caused appalling carnage. Dundee himself was struck by a musket ball and died after the battle.

Running at your opponent to unbalance him is an elementary form of attack which can be observed in any school playground. Carried out by a mass of men, it is a dangerously uncontrolled operation, and from earliest antiquity commanders of formed bodies of troops insisted on slowing down an advance to a measured pace. Charging at the run was thus the mark of lightly armed, untrained forces—of tribesmen rather than soldiers—and it was completely unfamiliar to the professional armies of European warfare. It was startling to be faced with such attack in the era of muskets and drill, very alarming to learn that it could be so devastatingly effective.

At the run or at the walk, the object was to pierce the enemy's line in order to attack his soldiers' unprotected flank and rear. No troops can stand up to this, hence the slaughter when the effort was successful; on the other hand, if the line remained unbroken, the attackers suffered heavily when they turned away to break off.

It has been suggested that the technique of the charge in its modern form was introduced by Montrose's ally, Alasdair MacColla, who had used it in the battle of Laney in Coleraine in 1642. Before field artillery came into general use, the critical moment for an attacking force occurred when its advance brought it within effective musket range, perhaps 100 to 150 yards, particularly if the enemy was steady, well drilled and, by 'platoon firing' in sequence, able to produce a sustained fire. By their appearance, their war cries and their reputation, Highlanders were often able to unsteady their opponents and reduce the danger of a succession of ordered volleys, while the sheer speed of their advance carried them through the first—and often only—volley with an acceptable proportion of casualties. Their own muskets were used to fire a single volley some thirty or forty yards from the enemy and were then immediately thrown down. The Highlanders burst through the cloud of black-powder smoke, broadsword drawn, dirk in the left hand and targe on the left fore-arm, while their enemy was reloading or fixing their bayonets.

General Hawley, whose forces were overwhelmed by such a charge at Falkirk in 1746, described how the Highlanders altered formation as they charged, from line—to minimise casualties from musket fire—to bunches or clusters of a dozen or so at the moment of impact, to achieve penetration of the enemy line. It was a 'double or quits' tactic which may have been an attraction to the Highlander, coupled with its opportunities for individual valour. The charge either won a battle there and then, or it was all over; to withdraw, re-group and charge again was psychologically as well as tactically so difficult as to be impossible.

*   *   *

Leven's Regiment did not disgrace itself at Killiecrankie and indeed was honoured by the City of Edinburgh for its steadfast behaviour. But, in the aftermath of that rout, the palm must be awarded to the Cameronian Regiment. It was raised in the same year as Leven's, 1689, and for the same purpose of countering Jacobite reluctance to accept William of Orange and his wife Mary (James II's daughter) as sovereigns of Scotland. Since the ousted regime had persecuted Covenanters, it was logical for the authorities to seek recruits in an area with strong covenanting sympathies, so a commission to raise a regiment was granted to the Earl of Angus. He was not yet twenty but had the merit of being the son of the Marquess of Douglas whose large estates lay in the south-west. It was stipulated that the men of Angus's Regiment should have a 'minister of their own persuasion' in addition to the usual Church of Scotland chaplain, and that each company should be provided with an elder.

A celebrated field preacher, Richard Cameron, had been the leader of a group of afflicted Covenanters until he was killed at Airds Moss in 1680, and his sect was known after him. Cameronians formed the nucleus of Angus's Regiment and from an early date gave their name to it. Their memories of field conventicles, when the word was preached on a lonely moorland in peril of surprise by the dragoons, led to the Cameronian tradition of going armed to church parades, with sentries posted outside during the service.

On Dundee's death after Killiecrankie, the victorious Highlanders were commanded by Colonel Cannon who proved incapable of exploiting the victory. He advanced on Dunkeld, which was held by Angus's Regiment or Cameronians. They had only received a couple of months' training, but in a remarkable feat of arms they not only held the little town against furious assaults but inflicted such losses on the Jacobites that the rising collapsed.

Plate 6
Figure 16
A grenadier of the regiment is shown in Figure 16, some ten years after the action at Dunkeld, when the regiment was fighting on the Continent in Marlborough's wars. It is recorded that their lining and facing colour was white at that time, though it was altered to yellow fairly early in the eighteenth century. The red coat is now worn open to the waist, with narrow lapels of the facing colour which also appears on the cuffs; the open coat exposed the upper part of the waistcoat. His grenadier cap is well on the way to assuming its eventual mitre shape; he carries a capacious pouch on his waistbelt for the grenades.

His breeches are still grey, but he wears a new form of leg protection. Marlborough's campaigns against the French, first under William and then Queen Anne, provided the British army's introduction to Flanders mud, against which two pairs of stockings (a coarse pair pulled over a thinner) were no protection. Spatterdashes or gaiters were improvised out of heavy cloth or canvas, as illustrated; they not only protected the legs from mud and wet but in dry weather prevented the soldier being crippled by loose stones in his shoes. Like so many articles of dress, something which in origin was strictly utilitarian became stylised, and very soon gaiters, white or black, were to form a showy part of full-dress uniform.

III: EIGHTEENTH CENTURY

The early years of the eighteenth century saw considerable changes in dress and equipment, partly due to lessons learned in Marlborough's wars when British troops fought as part of an international army, and in part due to the accession of George I in 1714. Hanoverian military experience must have been at variance with the comparatively haphazard organization of the army in Britain, and a long and often uphill struggle began to impose uniformity in dress against the caprices of colonels who were to some degree the proprietors of their regiments.

Some alterations were the effect of fashion in civilian dress. Hats, for instance, adopted the civilian mode of the tricorn or three-pointed shape, achieved by turning up three sides of the brim. In the army the tricorn was usually worn with one of its points over the left eye, with tape or braid round the brim and a button or clasp on the left-hand turn-up. This was an obvious location for an ornament, so it was behind this button that the cockade was fixed. It looks in some contemporary pictures like a bow or knot of black ribbon, but the usual form was a small rosette. It was worn by Hanoverian soldiers, and its adoption is usually attributed to George I's influence; Lawson points out that references exist to a black cockade being worn by some regiments from 1700 and that it was worn by several French corps. In his view there was nothing specifically Hanoverian about it, unlike the Elector of Hanover's device of a white horse and the words NEC ASPERA TERRENT (Don't be dismayed by difficulties). Both badge and motto appeared in British uniform well into the nineteenth century.

Hair was generally allowed to grow long at the back, and 'clubbed' at the nape of the neck i.e. gathered in a thick plait which was often tucked up under the hat or grenadier cap. Unfortunately the infantry depicted in *A Representation of the Cloathing of His Majesty's Household and of all the Forces upon the Establishment of Great Britain and Ireland* (1742) are shown full face, so one cannot tell if their hair is cut short in a sort of page-boy bob like that of the dragoons or grown long and clubbed.

Plate 7   The private of the 1st Foot (Royals) in Figure 17, about 1720, still wears a
Figure 17 full-skirted and almost knee-length red coat, the pattern of which was soon to change. In the 1730s, it became the practice to fasten back the skirts of the coat

26

on either side, producing a 'cutaway' effect and revealing the lining where the coat was folded back (see Figure 19). The 1st by now had blue linings and facings like other royal regiments, which also wore blue breeches. Unusually, the 1st are recorded as wearing red breeches in 1720. It is of course true that colonels were allowed (or at least took) considerable latitude over regimental dress, and equally true that changes in uniform never came into effect immediately or simultaneously throughout the army; existing uniform had to be worn out. The soldier had a new coat every year, the old one being cut down to make a waistcoat and, sometimes, spare breeches, which might account for the non-regulation breeches in this case.

He still carries a sword as his personal weapon, in addition to a bayonet. The latter was no longer the plug type which put the musket out of action but a ring or socket bayonet, adopted from the French. Its weight when fixed must have made the musket even more inaccurate, but at least it could still be fired.

Improvements in equipment did not extend to the soldier's totally inadequate footwear. In his campaigning kit an infantryman carried spare soles and heels to enable the regimental cobbler to carry out repairs, but the shoes themselves were simply leather foot coverings, with no distinction between left and right feet. As late as 1768 in his *System for the Compleat Interior Management and Oeconomy of a Battalion of Infantry*, Captain Bennet Cuthbertson insists 'that the men do not always wear their shoes on the same feet, but that they change them day about, to prevent their running crooked'.

The Royal Regiment of Scots Dragoons became in 1708 the (2nd) Royal North British Dragoons, with their sobriquet of The Greys well established. Figure 18 shows a grenadier trooper of about 1720, with the blue facings and lining to his coat and the blue breeches of a royal regiment, and wearing a grenadier cap. It is not clear when the whole regiment, not just the grenadier troop, wore these caps—perhaps around 1730; in 1768 they were ordered to wear a bearskin grenadier cap in place of the mitre-shaped cloth cap. The caps, with all their embroidery, were expensive and in bad weather they were protected by covers— a complication which became increasingly necessary throughout the army as headgear grew ever more ornate.

Plate 7
Figure 18

The shoulder knot worn by troopers consisted of a white plaited cord with small white-metal points. It was worn by all ranks in cavalry and dragoon regiments, though for officers it was a more elaborate affair, but in infantry regiments it was the rank badge of a corporal. In 1764, changes were made which were embodied in the Clothing Warrant of 1768. Officers and men of mounted units were to wear an epaulette on the left shoulder in place of the shoulder knot, and the waistcoats and breeches of the Royal North British Dragoons were altered from blue to white.

The Scotch Regiment of Foot Guards or the Regiment of Scotch Guards was entitled the Third Regiment of Foot Guards in 1712, and so remained until

Plate 7
Figure 19

1831. They had retained their white facings until 1707, when they were changed to blue, and also wore blue breeches until at least 1742, if one can rely on a hand-coloured facsimile of the *Cloathing Book*, in the Scottish United Services Museum. The private of the regiment shown in Figure 19, about 1740, wears these blue breeches. Coloured breeches, whether blue for royal regiments or red for others, were not a success because they were difficult to clean and after washing they became a dingy, muddy colour. Instead of reverting to the old grey, the army chose white breeches instead, on the ground that they kept their smartness longer, and by the 1760s they had been adopted by all regiments.

His coat has the skirts fastened back in the comparatively new style. The original reason for this was a practical one, in that it was more comfortable on the line of march than to have coat tails flapping against the legs. The skirts were held back by a hook and eye, so that it was simple enough in bad weather to unhook the skirts, to protect the thighs. Soon the fastening became an ornamental clasp, often in the shape of a grenade for grenadiers and for fusilier regiments. The lapels of the coat were permanently buttoned back, showing the lining and also the top of the waistcoat. The latter was still long, with deep pockets to make up for the fact that the coat pockets were hidden in the turned-back skirts.

It had become the mode to edge coat and cuffs, waistcoat and pockets with 'lace'. This was tape, usually white and with one or more twists of coloured thread running through it in a pattern peculiar to the regiment. The same lace was used to make 'loops' or tabs, variously shaped, on the lapels; on these loops the buttons were mounted and button-holes inserted.

The colour of the various regiments' linings and facings, and the pattern of the lace used for loops and edging, were gradually systematised. It was not until the Clothing Warrant of 1768, however, that these cherished distinctions were codified; most were in existence in 1742, and almost certainly long before that date.

The private in Figure 19 is wearing white gaiters secured under the knee with a dark grey ribbon, which later became a strap. The implication is that gaiters cannot have been buttoned very tightly up the outside of the leg.

Plate 8
Figure 20

The private in Figure 20 of the 21st Regiment or Royal North British Fuziliers wears the grenadier cap worn by all ranks in fusilier regiments. Its height offered a good field for ornament, and the resulting proliferation of colours, badges and mottoes was carefully regulated in the 1768 Warrant. The 21st had a particularly intricate design. The tall front was blue, edged white, and carried a white St Andrew's cross and star, in the centre of which was another saltire cross within a green circle of St Andrew; on either side of this central design were embroidered red scrolls. The little flap or frontlet was an important element in a grenadier cap, often carrying the white horse of Hanover. For the 21st, it was blue like the front, but with a white border edged either side in red and lettered 'Royal

Fuziliers'; in the centre of the flap appeared a thistle in purple and green. No wonder cap covers were worn in wet or dusty weather.

Their lace, too, was unusually ornate, with a yellow line on a white ground and a blue zig-zag line within that. The 21st had been made a royal regiment after the Treaty of Utrecht in 1713, hence the blue facings and lining. The privilege of carrying an individual design on grenadier caps was restricted to royal regiments and the six 'Old Corps'; the latter included the 21st, which was thus doubly entitled to the distinction.

The soldier in Figure 20, as in 19, carries the standard infantry weapons of the day—musket, socket bayonet and sword. The musket was an improvement on that used in Marlborough's campaigns at the beginning of the century. Still a flintlock, it was a very well balanced firearm with a better designed lock mechanism which somewhat reduced the chance of a misfire; a brush and pricker to clean the pan and touch-hole were attached to the waistbelt or to the tongue of the shoulder-belt. Its barrel at this date was forty-six inches long, reduced to forty-two in the 1750s; unlike muskets of the previous century of which the stocks were often painted black, the 'Brown Bess' had a stock stained brown.

The sword was already an anachronism for the infantryman; with his seventeen-inch bayonet, he did not need another hand weapon. A rather querulous order was issued in 1724 conveying the king's insistence that NCOs and men should carry swords. They did not, and the 1768 Warrant gave ground: 'All the Serjeants of the Regiment, and the whole Grenadier Company to have Swords. The Corporals and Private Men of the Battalion Companies (excepting the Regiment of Royal Highlanders) to have no Swords.'

Highland regiments have always been exceptions to general rules and in more respects than the carrying of swords. The Black Watch is the senior Highland regiment, though many years younger than the Scottish regiments described so far. In 1739, it was decided to form a regular army unit from the existing Independent Companies and May 1740 saw the first parade of the Highland Regiment or 43rd Regiment of Foot, which in 1749 was re-numbered the 42nd.

There had been a long tradition of trying to police the Highlands by means of locally-recruited companies, paid and armed by the Crown, but it was said that the resulting drop in blackmail (protection money paid as insurance against cattle-lifting) was because the most accomplished cattle thieves were members of the companies, operating on their own account. The companies or watches had been disbanded several times, most recently after their ineffectiveness had been exposed during the Jacobite Rising of 1715. Six new companies were raised in 1725 by General Wade, a bold step; but as Commander in Chief in Scotland he was in a position to supervise closely their organization and operations.

The old companies had each been attached for administrative purposes to one of the regiments stationed in Scotland. They had not been uniformed by the government, the men's status being denoted by a badge. This was not only economical but practical, since no better dress than the belted plaid could have been devised for the almost roadless Highland country they patrolled. In 1709, the Commissioners for Clothing of the Army had observed: 'there is a peculiar Cloathing for the three Highland Companies in North Britain, not at all Military but like the Cloathing of the Natives there'. Wade wisely made no attempt to alter the dress in 1725, although he ordered the commanders of his six new Independent Companies, scattered across the Highlands, to 'take care to provide a plaid clothing and bonnet in the Highland dress for non-commissioned officers and soldiers belonging to their companies, the plaid of each company to be as near as they can of the same sort or colour'. This implies that officers wore a tartan of their choice, that tartans were woven in such variety that uniformity of sett and colour was only approximate; and that even this limited degree of standardisation could only be achieved within a single company's area of operation and recruitment.

There is no evidence that the Independent Companies were issued with the short red jacket which was to become regimental wear – probably not if it is true that the nickname of *An Freiceadan Dubh* or Black Watch derives from the contrast of their appearance with that of the 'redcoats'. This derivation is disputed by those who claim that the name was an abusive reference to the Companies' role of suppressing blackmail. In either case, the regiment was not known by this name in the late eighteenth century, for Boswell in his enthusiasm for all things Highland would certainly have used it in his journal when he described their arrival at Edinburgh Castle in 1775. Instead, he refers to the Royal Highland Regiment (which it became in 1758) and the Highland Watch. It was not until 1861 that the Black Watch, as an honourable distinction, was added to their title.

Plate 8   The corporal of the regiment in Figure 21 is based on the *Cloathing Book* and
Figure 21 on one of Bowles's 'Mutineer' drawings (see page 34). The most distinctive feature of his dress, as a regular soldier, is of course the belted plaid of a tartan variously known as the government pattern, the government sett and the military pattern. Its origin is the subject of much controversy, as is the question of whether it was worn by the Independent Companies before they were embodied as the 43rd. It seems to have been a new tartan, and its dark blue, black and green sett, sometimes with a slight variation, became the tartan of a succession of regiments as well as forming the basis for several so-called clan or family tartans.

One very unlikely theory of its genesis is that any distinguishing overstripes were removed from the tartans of the individual Company commanders, to produce a sort of lowest common denominator; another is that it was invented from scratch because the first colonel, the Earl of Crawford, was a Lowlander. A third theory, advanced by Colonel M. M. Haldane, is that it was 'adapted from an old sett in common use all over the Highlands, since it is the basis of many tartans which only differ by additional stripes of brighter colours, and as such would be suitable to a regiment recruited throughout the Highlands'. This is perhaps related to yet another theory, that the sett, if not the colours, of the government pattern was derived from the Stewart worn since 1713 or 1714 by the Royal Company of Archers, the King's Bodyguard in Scotland.

The corporal wears a red jacket, short because the normal infantry coat would not accommodate the folds of a belted plaid. It had no collar or lapel, the buff lining and facing showing only at the throat and cuffs; a lapel was soon introduced. (Buff was a rather vague official description and ranged from cream to pale brown, to judge from extant examples.) The shoulder knot indicates his rank. His head-dress is a flat blue bonnet; its toorie may have been red, more likely blue, and it was probably garnished with a ribbon threaded through openings round the brim, which could be tightened and knotted at the back. This ribbon was later of red material, and was the origin of the familiar diced rim of the bonnet.

His diced hose are cut from cloth, not knitted; 'plaid for hose' is a frequent entry in clothing lists. The Bowles print shows sporran (a leather pouch with an ornamental top), dirk and pistol in addition to the broadsword and bayonet, although, in the *Cloathing Book*, the private has a pouch attached to the centre of his waistbelt but no sporran, dirk or pistol. The basket-hilted broadsword was only carried, as far as infantry was concerned, by Highland troops; its name did not imply any abnormal width, just that—unlike the backsword—it was edged on two sides, designed for slashing and not thrusting. The dirk, with a blade of some fifteen inches, and the pistol were both normal Highland accoutrements as was the targe or small round shield which men of the new regiment in its early years were permitted to acquire at their own expense.

The Scottish pistol was a very unusual firearm, being of all-metal construction. It was manufactured in the Lowlands, at Doune in particular, mainly for the Highland market, although the workmanship was of so fine a quality that examples found their way to the French court. It was regarded as an integral feature of Highland dress and therefore became a government issue to Highland regiments. 'Issue' pistols came to be made in London and Leith, with wooden butts, but superbly engraved all-metal pistols were often purchased by officers. Engraved or plain, they were fitted with a catch to hang at chest height from a narrow shoulder strap. The long trigger, with a bulbous terminal, had no trigger-guard and the butt was finished in a decorative shape—fish-tail, lobed, heart and, for most Highland regiments, the scroll or ram's horn, with a pricker screwed into the butt between the incurved 'horns'. A metal ramrod lay under the barrel. The overall length of the pistol was about fifteen inches.

The private of a battalion company of the 26th Foot (Cameronians) in Figure **Plate 8** 22 is based on the 1742 *Cloathing Book*. The regimental facings had by this date **Figure 22** been changed from white to yellow, a popular colour amongst Scottish regiments and with at least as many variations as buff. The 1768 Warrant listed deep yellow, bright yellow, pale yellow (worn by the 26th) and 'philamort yellow' (*feuille* *morte*). Since he is not in the grenadier company, he wears a tricorn hat with a yellow trim. The loops on the lapels, which are now wider, and the edges of the pockets are not decorated with regimental lace, as was to become the rule. Waistcoats and breeches were still red, and his grey-white stockings are visible at the knee above his white gaiters. His waistbelt and shoulder-belt are buff leather. All muskets were now fitted with a sling, not just those of grenadiers and fusiliers; it was observed later in the century that the sole purpose of the ordinary infantryman's musket sling appeared to be for making a noise during arms drill, for he never carried his musket slung.

The battle of Culloden in 1746 put paid to the Forty Five and any Jacobite hope of a Stewart restoration. The chances of success had been better in 1715 when Scotland was disillusioned with the recent Union between its parliament and that at Westminster, and unenthusiastic about the accession of the Elector of Hanover as George I; but the Fifteen had petered out as the result of indecisive leadership. Thirty years later support for the Jacobite cause had dwindled save amongst some clans in the western Highlands and in the hearts of die-hard Stewart adherents. Even so, Louis XV's plan of supporting a rising with troops and money was not ill-conceived, since the greater part of the British army was on the Continent fighting the French. In the event, a storm shattered the French fleet and the expedition was abandoned. Against all advice, Prince Charles Edward, son of the Old Pretender, landed in Moidart with a handful of followers and raised his father's standard—an attempt foredoomed to failure, say some historians; one that might have succeeded, according to others, if the Jacobite army had advanced on London instead of abandoning their southward march at Derby.

Highland tactics and equipment had altered little since the days of Montrose a century earlier, except for the fact that there were no longer bowmen in the Jacobite ranks. But there had been a major change in Highland dress with the introduction of the 'little kilt' or *feileadh beag*, anglicised as phillibeg—another subject of hot dispute, for exactly how and when it was adopted is not at all clear. It was stated confidently in the eighteenth century that an Englishman called Rawlinson in 1728 suggested to the Highlanders working for him in Lochaber that they would find it convenient to turn the plaid into two separate garments, a cloak and a kilt. It has been retorted that such an obvious step needed no suggestion from an outsider, and that the adaptation of the belted plaid was a natural development. However it evolved, the wearing of the kilt spread quickly and widely throughout the Highlands, although it should be noted that the belted plaid or *feileadh mhor* remained the regimental dress for years to come, even after the kilt had been accepted as undress uniform.

Plate 9   The Jacobite soldier of Figure 23 is largely based on David Morier's well
Figure 23 known painting in the Royal Collection, of an incident in the battle of Culloden. It was painted for the victor, and Morier's patron, the Duke of Cumberland,

with Jacobite prisoners as models. One must assume that the tartans are accurately depicted—Morier also painted for Cumberland a series of pictures of grenadiers of different regiments, the whole purpose of which was to record faithfully details of their uniforms. It is remarkable that the setts of the tartans worn as jacket, waistcoat, kilt or trews are all different, even on the same man. No belted plaid is shown; and as one would expect, the charging Highlanders are shown in every case but one as having cast off the separate plaid to free the sword arm.

The white cockade can be seen in our Jacobite's bonnet, the distinguishing badge in the absence of a uniform dress. There were soldiers of the government army in Highland dress, and it is said that after the battle a wounded man who had lost his bonnet was asked by Cumberland to which side he belonged; his reply, 'to the Prince', was his instant death warrant. The story, which takes several forms, underlines the problem of recognition when there was no uniform.

The impact of the charge and the fearful slashing cuts of the broadsword had served the Jacobites well in their brilliant successes at Preston Pans and Falkirk, but at Culloden everything was against them. They were exhausted and hungry, the Prince's (or his Irish adviser O'Sullivan's) choice of a flat, open moor as a battlefield was disastrous, and Cumberland could break up a charge with artillery and musket fire. In addition, he had been training his troops, if it came to close quarters, to ignore the man who came straight at them and instead to lunge with the bayonet at the unshielded side of the man on the attacker's left.

Of Cumberland's fifteen infantry battalions, three were Scottish, the 1st (second battalion), the 21st and the 25th. The 1st (St Clair's) and 21st maintained a heavy musketry fire in the first line, while the 25th never had to fire a shot. In addition, there were companies of the Argyll Militia and a company of Loudon's Highlanders, a second regular Highland regiment in the course of formation in 1745, which played a role in the closing stages of the battle. The Argyll Militia are thought to have worn tartan of the government pattern, like the 43rd. Eighteen additional Independent Companies were raised in the Highlands to meet the crisis, most not uniformed until after Culloden although armed and paid by the government, and with the distinguishing badge of a red cross saltire on the black cockade.

Plate 9
Figure 24
A grenadier of St Clair's, the 1st, is shown in Figure 24. Perhaps it was as well that St Clair's did not receive the Jacobite charge, because they, and three other of Cumberland's battalions at Culloden, had been broken by it at Falkirk. As a soldier of a royal regiment, his lining and facings are blue, with white lace (by 1768, the lace of the 1st had become white 'with a blue double worm' i.e. a chain effect). His grenadier cap, with a white tuft securing the bag to its top, shows the full development of the mitre shape. The front carried the royal cypher and crown, ringed with Scotland's motto NEMO ME IMPUNE LACESSIT; on the front flap appeared the white horse and the usual NEC ASPERA TERRENT. At the back of the grenadier or fusilier cap there was another, much smaller, plate which bore the regiment's 'rank', its number.

On their shoulder-belts, grenadiers carried a match-case, originally supplied to ignite the fuse of a grenade before throwing it. In fact, grenades had ceased to be carried and did not re-appear until 1915, but the match-case continued to be a grenadier distinction.

Despite the wet and stormy weather of that April day at Culloden, it is probable that grenadiers did wear their ornate and costly caps, since one of their functions was to make the wearer appear more formidable.

The 43rd were not in Scotland during the Forty Five. In 1743, they had been earmarked for service in Flanders, but the authorities failed to explain to the men what had been intended and a considerable body mutinied in the belief that they were to be shipped to the West Indies; Bowles's 'Mutineer' drawings were made at the time of the subsequent courts-martial. This was the first of a number of similar incidents involving Highland regiments, the result of bad administration and bad communication with largely Gaelic-speaking soldiers. In May 1745, the regiment distinguished itself at the battle of Fontenoy, but when with other units it was withdrawn from Flanders because of the Rising, it was prudently stationed in Kent since many of the officers and men had relatives in the Jacobite army. Three new companies then being raised in Scotland for the 43rd did take a minor part in the campaign.

Plate 10
Figure 25
By the 1750s, the date of Figure 25, the 43rd had been re-numbered the 42nd. The regiment had been ordered in 1747 to equip a grenadier company with caps of black bearskin—it may have been thought that the usual mitre-shaped cloth cap would look absurd with Highland dress. The grenadier in this illustration is based on Morier's paintings of 1751. The bearskin of the cap replaced the tall embroidered front of the conventional cap, but the little front-flap remained, red in this case and perhaps painted metal, perhaps embroidered cloth. His facings are buff, which was changed to blue after the 42nd became the Royal Highland Regiment of Foot.

Unlike the corporal of Figure 21, he wears a short coat with a fairly large turned-down collar, and his sporran is a plain leather purse. His sword-belt and waistbelt are of black leather; it is noteworthy that Morier painted him with a bayonet hanging from his waistbelt as though it were a dirk, and with no pistol. The dirk may have been left out because it was a personal possession, not a government issue, but the omission of a pistol, which was an issue, is surprising, unless only men of battalion companies were so equipped.

The most interesting aspect of Morier's painting is the tartan, which is the government pattern with a thin red overstripe. This differentiation is said to have been introduced by Lord John Murray, who became colonel in 1745, probably for the grenadier company alone, though this is far from certain. Another theory is that only the grenadiers wore the belted plaid with the red stripe, while the whole regiment wore the kilt in this pattern in undress uniform. In the *Scottish Gael* (1831, but based on notes made earlier), Logan writes: 'It appeared to me very un-uniform in this regiment, that both patterns should be worn indifferently'. He is not always reliable, but this passage certainly reads like direct knowledge and not hearsay. The red overstripe appears in an aquatint based on a contemporary drawing by Hamilton Smith of a 42nd grenadier in 1812, so it had a long life. The same difference seems to have been added to the government sett for the tartan of Loudon's Highlanders in 1745, to judge from Alan Ramsay's portrait of the Earl of Loudon in uniform; this may have preceded Lord John Murray's decision. Loudon's, as the only other Highland regiment, was also entitled to equip the grenadiers with fur caps, a short-lived distinction since the regiment was disbanded in 1748.

The services rendered to the Crown by troops wearing traditional Highland dress led directly to the exemption of the military from the stringent provisions of the Act of 1746 '. . . for restraining the use of the Highland dress'. It banned 'the plaid, philabeg or little kilt, trowse, shoulder belt or any part whatsoever of what peculiarly belongs to the Highland garb; . . . no tartan or parti-coloured plaid or stuff shall be used for great coats or for upper coats.' Unlike the disarming order for Highland counties, the Act applied to the whole of Scotland, although it was enforced far more rigorously in the Highlands, with penalties of six months imprisonment for a first offence and seven years transportation for a second to 'any of H.M. plantations beyond the seas'. Until its repeal in 1782, it was only in one of the growing number of Highland regiments that a Highlander could bear arms or wear his native dress, and it is doubtful if Highland dress, or even tartan, would otherwise have survived a generation's proscription. The fact that it could still legally be worn by a section of the community—and with distinction in three continents—encouraged its wear in parts of Scotland where the Act was less strictly applied. David Allan's painting of *A Highland Wedding at Blair Atholl 1780* displays a wide variety of tartans as plaid, kilt and even knee-breeches with only one Highland soldier enjoying the party.

The clothing of the 3rd Regiment of Foot Guards was altered in 1768, although not as part of the very detailed Royal Warrant of that year which laid down 'the Regulation of the Colours, Clothing, etc. of the Marching Regiments of Foot'; the three regiments of Foot Guards were always dealt with separately, as part of Plate 10 the Household troops. The sergeant in Figure 26 is dressed in accordance with Figure 26 an order of April 1768, and several points call for comment. The lining and facing of the coat were no longer the same colour, since a white lining was standard and came to be so for regiments of foot also. He wears a single epaulette of gold lace, indicating that he held his rank in a battalion company; grenadier sergeants wore two, while a corporal had a single silver epaulette. His coat no longer has voluminous slashed cuffs but the new 'small round' pattern. The order laid down that buttons and loops were to be 'set on two and two'; it was not until 1774 that buttons in groups of three—still a mark of Scots Guards uniform—were introduced. The flaps of his coat pockets were purely ornamental since they were sewn down, the access to the pocket being by means of a slit in the inside lining.

His waistcoat is now white, although corporals and privates of the regiment still wore red waistcoats at this time; before long, all waistcoats throughout the army were white, as were breeches. Apart from his epaulette, his rank is shown by the halberd (which since 1725 had also been carried by corporals of the Foot Guards) and by his crimson worsted sash. The sergeants of Line regiments were ordered by the 1768 Warrant to wear such a sash with a broad stripe of the regiment's facing colour running through it. His hat is the familiar tricorn but the shape was changing; the front point was now much less marked—a stage towards the evolution of the bicorn hat with only two points.

Under the hat he wears his hair plaited or clubbed and powdered. Cuthbertson, already quoted, suggested that a plait, with a 'bow knot at the tie', was preferable to a queue because the latter greased the back of the coat. There was thus a choice of styles until, in 1796, it was ordered that all officers and men were to wear their hair queued, to be tied slightly below the upper part of the coat collar and to be ten inches in length 'including one inch of hair to appear below the binding'. A year earlier the use of hair powder had at last been abolished, to the relief of the rank and file to whom it must have been an intolerable nuisance. The 'List of Necessaries to be provided for the Foot Soldier out of his pay' included a powdering bag and puff once every three years, at 1s. 6d.; two combs at 6d. each; and grease and powder for the hair, 3s. per year. Men should powder their hair, says Cuthbertson, every Sunday and whenever they paraded for duty. Officers followed civilian fashion in wearing either their own hair or else a short wig, usually tied with a black ribbon at the nape of the neck. Hair was shaved or close-cropped under a wig, so pictures of officers who have lost their hat and wig in action show a bald pate.

During the Seven Years War (1755–1763) half a dozen new Highland regiments were raised, all being disbanded after it was over; in the execution of Pitt's policy of attacking France through her colonies, some of these units fought in North America, others in Europe. One of the first to be formed, in 1757, was the old 77th Foot or Montgomerie's Highlanders in which the young Hugh Montgomerie, a relation of the colonel, was commissioned as lieutenant. The regiment was engaged in the capture of Fort du Quèsne (renamed Pittsburgh) and of St John's, Newfoundland, and also in operations against the Cherokee Indians, before its disbandment in 1763. The officer in Figure 27 is based upon Copley's portrait, in the Scottish National Portrait Gallery, of Montgomerie, painted many years later after he had become 12th Earl of Eglinton in 1796. By then he had left the regular army, had served in the Argyll and Western Fencibles (raised in 1788) and had been appointed colonel of the West Lowland Fencibles in 1793, but for this portrait he chose to be painted in the uniform of his first regiment against a background scene of warfare with Indian braves. The 77th wore a belted plaid

Plate 10
Figure 27

of the government pattern tartan, and had green facings with silver lace for officers, as in the portrait, while the Argyll and Western Fencibles had yellow facings and the West Lowland Fencibles wore trews.

The painting, so much later in date, could not be wholly accurate. The short coat, for instance, would have had slashed cuffs and probably not the round cuffs depicted, which were authorised in 1768, although it is true to say that regulations frequently gave official sanction to changes that had been already made. The bonnet certainly is of a pattern that came into being after the disbandment of the 77th which would have worn a version of the old flat bonnet, possibly with a stiffened rim to show off the dicing. By the date of the portrait, the bonnet was cocked to give it height, above a taller rim, and instead of a single feather or strip of bearskin, a bunch of black feathers now decorated it.

He is correctly shown as wearing two epaulettes, a distinction peculiar to all officers of Highland regiments. His tartan has a somewhat lighter green than was usual in the government pattern, but this may well be an accurate rendering of the actual weave. It will be noticed that by the 1790s the full belted plaid was being replaced by the half-plaid, with a much reduced bulk round the hips. His silver-chased pistol, with ram's-horn butt, would have been purchased privately, as would the ornate dirk with silver-mounted knife and fork set into the scabbard. There is no evidence that so highly decorated a sporran was worn about 1760, or that it could have been a regimental pattern. Even if the young Montgomerie had owned such costly possessions as a junior officer of the 77th, he would never have worn them in action. There is one surprising omission in the painting—he is not wearing the usual officer's sash.

On disbandment, officers and men were offered the choice of transferring to another regiment, often with a bounty as an inducement, instead of being shipped home to Britain or—in the case of those serving in North America—becoming settlers with a grant of land. Many of those who chose the latter course rejoined the army in 1775, on the outbreak of the War of American Independence, to form the Royal Highland Emigrants, a corps which according to Lawson appears to have worn the government sett with a red overstripe. One would like to know, if that is the case, when the tartan was shipped to America, and whether it was specially woven since it was not the standard pattern; it is not until much later in the century that weavers' accounts are available, and even they are uninformative on the pattern of tartan supplied.

Minorca oscillated between French and British control during the eighteenth century but in the interval between the Seven Years War and the War of American Independence it was occupied by Britain. The 25th Foot was stationed there from 1769 to 1775 and, with soldiers from other regiments of the garrison, they form the subject of a series of oil paintings and watercolours, now in the National Army Museum and the Scottish United Services Museum. The pictures show a remarkable variety of dress, as many commentators have pointed out—

something which underlines how long officially out-dated styles could linger on. The next three subjects are based upon these Minorca paintings.

We have already noted the existence of pipers in Lowland regiments, uniformed in exactly the same way as the rank and file. The piper of the 25th in Figure 28, however, is dressed in full Highland garb, a fact which demonstrates that Highland dress was accepted by 1770 as a military norm, and also that as a consequence it was believed, even outside the Highlands, that belted plaid or kilt was a more appropriate dress for a piper than a long coat and breeches. It is impossible to be certain about the dark tartan he wears; it may well have been the government sett since it is most unlikely that the colonel at that date, Lord George Lennox, had a personal tartan, although he was of Stewart descent. The piper's bonnet, in contrast to the anachronism of Montgomerie's in Figure 27, has a continuous red rim, not diced, and is not cocked to give it height.

In an Inspection Return of 1768, it was noted that the 25th 'have a bag-piper in the Band of Music', though there is no reference to his dress. If the Minorca piper were carried on the books as a bandsman, it would explain why his short coat is not red, but in reversed colours like that of a drummer in the same painting—yellow (which was the regiment's facing colour) with facings of red. His sleeves resemble those of the drummer in being decorated with lace chevrons of blue, yellow and red in a pattern of lines and circles quite different from the regimental lace, which employed the same colours in stripes on a white ground. As we shall see later, drummers' lace was always distinctive, while Highland regiments came to dress their pipers in special doublets. The colonel's piper in the illustration carries an elegant stand of ivory-fitted pipes and, interestingly, no sword, although the broadsword continued to be worn by pipers after it had been given up by rank and file. It has been noted that after 1768 only grenadiers and all ranks of the 42nd retained broadswords. An Inspection Report on the 42nd of 1775 reported that, according to their colonel, 'the Highlanders on several occasions declined using broadswords in America, that they all prefer bayonets, and that swords for the Battalion men ... are incumbrances'.

Uniform as well as equipment had suffered modification after the experience of campaigning in the climate and terrain of North America during the Seven Years War, the changes being most marked in the dress of the new 'light infantry'. Its success led to the formation within each battalion of another specialist company in addition to the grenadiers, a light company: the two were called the flank companies of the battalion. Light troops wore a more manageable uniform; the long coat was cut down to something like a short Highland jacket, long gaiters gave way to calf-length ones and tricorn hats were replaced by leather helmets of various designs, often decorated with a plume or a strip of fur. As usually happened, some adaptations of uniform were abandoned in peacetime while those that were retained were formalised.

The next subject taken from the Minorca paintings, Figure 29, is a light company officer of the 25th whose uniform reflects these changes. His short red coat is of course faced with the regimental 'deep yellow', and shows his white waistcoat. He wears short black gaiters, which rose to a slight point at the swell of the calf. His cap is unusual; it appears to be of leather, painted or laquered red, with black fur edging the crown and the small red front plate which was ornamented with the device of a thistle and NEMO ME IMPUNE LACESSIT. The profusion of black fur on his cap, and the oddity of his carrying a broadsword, are probably connected with the colonel's practice, we are told, of calling the light company his Highland company. This officer carries no spontoon, as do battalion company officers in the paintings, but his sash indicates his commissioned rank, the gorget that he is on duty.

In the Minorca pictures of the 25th all ranks, with very few exceptions, are shown wearing a little sprig of greenery in their hat or cap, for which no explanation has been offered. The 25th is one of the six 'Minden regiments' which commemorate their achievements at that battle in 1759 by wearing a rose in their hat on Minden Day. It is a tenable conjecture that, if roses were unobtainable in Minorca on 1 August, a sprig of leaves was substituted, and it would be natural for the colonel, when commissioning a set of paintings of his regiment, to have the 25th depicted celebrating their finest feat of arms.

Plate 11
Figure 30
The grenadier of the regiment in full dress, Figure 30, is taken from a watercolour, also painted in Minorca. The wearing of fur caps had been authorised for grenadiers of all regiments, not only Highland, and for fusilier regiments, in the 1768 warrant, but the 25th had received permission to adopt them three years before that, in addition to plain white waistcoat and breeches for officers and white breeches for the men. The cap is unusual in having no front plate, though a small plate at the back carried the regimental rank, XXV.

Men of the flank companies wore 'wings', at this period of regimental lace, with the object of making the shoulders look broader. But until they were stiffened and projected slightly, wings were very ineffective in doing this, to judge from the rather bottle-shouldered grenadier in the watercolour. He wears a purely ornamental match-case on his shoulder-belt and carries no sword, although a grenadier of the Buffs, also part of the garrison, is painted with a sword but no match-case. Match-cases were finally abolished in 1784.

His long black gaiters look as if they were in one piece, but in fact consisted of a black leather knee-shield and knee-length gaiter. The invaluable Cuthbertson recommends that the latter should be of stout grey linen, blacked, and that there should be 'a stiff leather top ... which buckles behind, above the calf, entirely covers the pan of the knee, defends it when kneeling ... and is a considerable addition to the good appearance of the leg.' The blacking introduced another complication for the infantryman when it was proposed that, like a cavalryman, he should wear white linen 'tops' over his knees to stop his white breeches being soiled. In 1784, it was recommended that these linen gaiters and leather tops should be replaced by black woollen cloth gaiters, with white-metal buttons, reaching just below the knee.

Note the difference in width between his two shoulder-belts. This is because one of them represents the old waistbelt from which the sword and bayonet were suspended. The waistbelt was constricting and uncomfortable for troops on the march, and they preferred to wear it over the free shoulder—a sensible practice which was at first tolerated and then enshrined in Dress Regulations in 1782. Two years later it was ordered that both shoulder belts must be of the same width, two inches.

It is hard to leave the 25th in Minorca without noting that Colonel Lord George Lennox had a furious row with the Governor over the infamous wine being provided for the troops. Additionally, in some units of the garrison wine was supplied, at a large profit, by the commanding officer. Lord George's complaint was in such terms that he was court-martialled and censured, but the Governor clearly thought some further action was demanded. He threw a Minorcan wine merchant into prison and was then successfully sued by him for £10,000 damages, on account of his imprisonment rather than the aspersion on the quality of his wine.

It was only a dozen years after the disbandment of the Highland regiments raised in the Seven Years War that the recruiting parties were out again with the outbreak of the War of American Independence. Many of these new units were in turn disbanded after the Treaty of Paris in 1783, only for the same pattern to be repeated when more regiments were formed after revolutionary France declared war on Britain in 1793. This alternation of recruitment and reduction accounts for the apparent confusion in the numbering of Highland regiments.

The 73rd was raised in 1777, largely in the Mackenzie territory of the northern Highlands, by Lord MacLeod, who as a young man had been out in the Forty Five; he was subsequently pardoned and had become a Lieutenant-General in the Swedish army. A second battalion was raised in the following year and formed part of the garrison during the three-year siege of Gibraltar, after which it was disbanded. The first battalion went to India in 1780, being re-numbered the 71st in 1786 and later becoming the Highland Light Infantry.

The regiment wore a distinctive tartan, the government sett with two overstripes, one of red and the other buff, which was the colour of the regimental facings. At some time before 1800 the overstripes were changed to one red and two white stripes. This may have been done in imitation of the 78th, raised in 1793 by Colonel Mackenzie of Seaforth, (see p. 53), since the 71st was also a Mackenzie regiment, or it may have been the other way round. The outcome at least is certain: the tartan worn by the two regiments (with a slight difference in the positioning of the white overstripes) became known as the Mackenzie and adopted as the 'clan tartan'.

Plate 12 Sketches exist of the Gibraltar garrison, on which Figure 31 is based—an
Figure 31 officer of the 2nd Battalion, the 73rd or Lord MacLeod's Highlanders. The

tartan of his half-plaid and kilt is the government sett with red and buff overstripes. Other pictures of the 73rd at Gibraltar show officers and men in the kilt, with no half-plaid. His short red coat is opened to show the frill of his shirt. Officers of the regiment wore silver lace and buttons, set on in two's, and his two epaulettes are therefore also silver. Unlike the picture of Montgomerie in Figure 27, he wears a sash over his left shoulder, but his dirk and sporran appear to be similar. The pistol, with a lobed and not a ram's-horn butt, is no longer carried on its own narrow shoulder strap but stuck into the waistbelt. His bonnet resembles Montgomerie's though it is not cocked so high in the crown.

The battalion sent to India adopted a different form of dress. In North America, Highland dress had on occasion been abandoned, sometimes due to lack of replacement uniform for worn-out kit; the belted plaid would be cut down to make a kilt, in turn replaced by trousers when it became unusable. There was also pressure to leave off the plaid on the ground of convenience. In his *British Military Uniforms 1768–96*, Strachan quotes a letter of 1781 written to HQ by Brigadier-General Allan MacLean, in Quebec: '. . . the 84th have tartan hose, plaids and bonnets. I am perfectly satisfied that bretches, hats and stockings are preferable for the men's healths in Canada in the winter season, but your excellency knows that soldiers are very ready to grumble, and that I dare not without an order from headquarters for that purpose, change the tartan hose, bonnet and plaid, into round hats, bretches and stockings . . .'. In India and the West Indies heat was naturally the reason for change, but loose trousers rather than breeches were adopted as an alternative to the kilt.

Plate 12
Figure 32 A form of tropical dress is shown in Figure 32, a battalion company man of the 73rd in India about 1785, just before the regiment became the 71st. The officers and men wore 'plaid jackets, linen waistcoats and long linen trousers . . . The kilts and hose long completely worn out'. The private's hat is conjectural in shape, although it is known that it was black; it may have been made of the usual felt, or of laquered straw. It was clearly unsatisfactory, for in 1787 instructions were issued for 'the four new Regiments for India' (74th, 75th, 76th and 77th) to wear white hats. These were quite high in the crown, built on a wicker framework—a forerunner of the later topi or sun-helmet. The white hat was to carry the regimental rank on a central button, which was possibly also the case with the earlier black hat. Arabic numerals were beginning to be used for this purpose in some regiments as an alternative to roman.

The white hat in its turn was rejected and troops in India reverted to a round black hat which, it was ordered, must be at least six inches high in the crown, with a brim of not less than four inches.

IV: THE FRENCH WARS: 1793–1815

The Duke of York and Albany, George III's second son, showed an early interest in the army, of which he became Commander in Chief in 1798, the only bishop to have held that appointment (thanks to his father's influence as Elector of Hanover, he became the titular Bishop of Osnaburg at the early age of one). He had proved a disastrous commander in the field, being soundly beaten by the French in three successive campaigns in Flanders, but he had realized that the British forces he led so ingloriously were ill-trained, badly officered and deplorably clothed and equipped, thanks to inefficient and corrupt administration. His career as Commander in Chief was interrupted by a major scandal over the sale of commissions by his mistress, but he did a great deal to put the organization of the army on a better footing.

Before becoming Commander in Chief he had employed the painter and engraver Edward Dayes to produce for him a series of watercolours of officers and men of various regiments, as David Morier had done a generation earlier for the Duke of Cumberland. They date from the early 1790s and are an invaluable guide to the final development of eighteenth-century uniform, before the great changes that came into effect in the course of the twenty-two year long war with France.

Plate 13
Figure 33 The officer of the 1st, Royal, Regiment in Figure 33 is based on Dayes's work. The most noticeable change is in the coat, which is now cut away at the hips instead of having long, full skirts buttoned back; the coat-tails reach the back of the knee. The lapels extend to the waist, emphasizing the curved cut of the coat front, open at the top to show the shirt frill and below the chest to reveal the waistcoat and his crimson sash, worn under the coat. The collar now stands up instead of being turned down; the collar, cuffs and lapels are blue, for a royal regiment. His sword-belt carries an oval gilt plate with the royal arms—this was a feature which became steadily larger and more ornate in the following century. Dayes may not have been accurate over the belt plate, for there are references to the 1st displaying the star of the Order of the Thistle on the plate at this time, with either 'Royal' or 'Royal Regiment'. Interestingly, Dayes shows the plural, 'Royals', on this officer's gorget, together with the royal arms.

The gorget has been noted already as the sign that an officer was on duty; it was a vestigial remnant of the piece of armour that protected the throat. At this period the gorget was gilt or silver according to the lace and buttons worn by officers in each regiment, and under the 1768 Warrant, it was engraved with the royal arms, the number of the regiment and its badge if it were entitled to one. Dayes's painting shows very clearly the blue ribbon on which it hung, with blue rosettes at the point of attachment.

His gold-laced hat, worn at an angle, is well on the way to becoming a bicorn. In it he wears a black cockade secured by a gold button, with a plume above it. Plumes had become fashionable in the previous decade, although it was not until 1797 that colours were laid down in regulations. In this case, Dayes shows a coloured or black tip to the white plume, but there seems to be no other reference to this. Finally, note his single epaulette. In 1791, it was laid down that, apart from Highland regiments, only field officers (colonels, lieutenant-colonels and majors) and officers of flank companies were to wear two.

By 1800 major changes had taken place. The black felt hat with its brim turned up in various styles was replaced by more practical headgear, at first for soldiers and soon for officers as well. The 'stove-pipe' hat or shako was a high-crowned, flat-topped cylinder made of leather, with a peak to shade the eyes. In front it carried a rectangular brass plate engraved with the regimental number and the royal cypher. It still retained a plume, though smaller than before, in colours which denoted a man's company and not his regiment—white for the grenadier company, green for the light company and white over red for battalion companies. Officers' plumes were of feathers, usually cut to make them stiffer, while those of the men were often worsted. The original stove-pipe hat was too heavy, and the material was changed from leather to felt.

Plate 13
Figure 34
The light company corporal of the 1st, about 1810, in Figure 34 is wearing this type of hat, which was soon to be replaced by another pattern of shako. His coat is short; in 1797, lapels had been abolished for other ranks, so the coat became single-breasted, still retaining loops of regimental lace. The facing colour was now to be seen on the stand-up collar, lace-edged and three inches high, and on the cuffs which were decorated with four buttons and loops. As a flank company NCO, his coat is decorated with wings, in this case of blue and white stripes with a white edging; the facing colour also appears on his shoulder straps, which have a narrow lace edge. Because the coat was worn buttoned, the waistcoat was invisible; it was still worn, with its long sleeves, under the coat on parade or on service, but without the coat it formed a fatigue jacket for dirty jobs.

It was a transitional period for leg-wear. Breeches and gaiters were still worn, the latter being of the short pattern for light companies, but they were evolving into one-piece trouser-gaiters, as worn by this corporal. Both were increasingly worn as parade dress, and on service overalls were issued which as the name implies were originally put on over the breeches. The logical step soon followed and overalls alone were worn, in effect as trousers. They were at first white, that being the colour of the breeches or trouser-gaiters they replaced, but in the course of the Peninsular War they became various shades of grey or blue-grey.

Plate 13
Figure 35 To complete the story of the 1st's dress during this period, Figure 35 shows an officer of the regiment, about 1815, wearing overalls. His crimson silk sash and the blue facings to his coat are almost the only resemblances to the uniform of his 1790s predecessor in Figure 33. The coat itself is an entirely new pattern. Coats with long tails were still worn in full dress, but on service it was a 'bum freezer' which in front stopped short at the waist. Unlike the soldier's coat, it was still double-breasted, and with lapels. It could be worn buttoned across as in the illustration; it could be worn with the lapels folded open, in which case it was secured at the front with hooks and eyes so that the lace loops of the two lapels formed continuous bars; or it could be worn with only the tops of the lapels turned back, to show two little triangles of the facing colour.

His shako is the new pattern which had been introduced in 1812 but was often called the Waterloo shako. The felt cylinder was now much lower in the crown, and to compensate a leather front was added, taller than the crown, to which an oval brass plate was fixed for number, badge, etc. The cockade and plume were moved from the front to the left, as they had been placed on the tricorn, but now an ornamental cord was fastened to the cockade button, looped down to the peak and up again at the other side of the shako, with a couple of tassels hanging down. This development stemmed from the grenadier's bearskin cap which by the end of the eighteenth century had been ornamented with such cords and tassels, usually either white or gold.

The practicality of an article of military dress is called into question when one finds that it has to be protected from weather. On wet days a black oilskin cover was worn over this shako, from which the plume could be removed. Waterloo was its swansong, for in 1815 a new pattern, the bell-topped shako, was authorised and came into use in most regiments the following year.

Figures 36, 37 and 38 illustrate types of dress in local defence forces. With its great firths and deeply-indented sea lochs, Scotland has an extensive coastline and has always been open to hostile landings from the sea. War against France meant fear of invasion, heightened by memories of French support for the Jacobites earlier in the century. The most important defence units in Scotland were fencible regiments, of which twenty-six were raised in the Highlands and another seventeen in the Lowlands in the second half of the eighteenth century. The exact number is debatable, for regiments were raised, reduced and re-formed; while some consisted only of a few companies, others had more than one battalion. Fencibles were raised only in time of war and were disbanded at the end of hostilities. Their terms of service at first stipulated that, unless they volunteered to do so, they would not be moved beyond the borders of Scotland except in the event of invasion; later this condition was varied to 'outside Europe'. Apart from this restriction, they resembled regular regiments in their recruitment, administration and equipment; their officers were appointed, and their commissions signed, by the king.

In contrast, Volunteer formations did not enjoy pay or army rank unless called out in an emergency for service, which was not to exceed six months. Volunteer bodies were raised all over Britain, mainly in cities, between 1779 and 1782 when many regular units were abroad and there were real fears of a French invasion.

The third form of local defence was the militia, which was based on a form of peacetime conscription, each county having to produce a quota of men who served for three years, doing company drills locally with an annual training period. The militia could only be embodied by royal proclamation, when it was to be paid on the same footing as the army. There was great indignation in Scotland in the latter part of the eighteenth century that there was no Scots militia, a slur, it was felt, on Scotland's loyalty. When eventually Militia Acts for Scotland were passed in 1797 and 1802, there was even more indignation and some rioting, because the system used to select the conscripts was resented as arbitrary.

Plate 14
Figure 36
Figure 36 represents Sir John Sinclair who raised the Rothesay and Caithness Fencibles (an extraordinary topographical conjunction) in 1794, with a second battalion a year later, both being disbanded in 1802. Some Highland fencibles wore the belted plaid, others, as in Raeburn's portrait of Sir John, in the National Gallery of Scotland, wore trews. These are real trews, not the tartan trousers that have usurped the name; with them he wears the 'big plaid', not the half-plaid which by then had been generally adopted. Both plaid and trews are the government-pattern tartan, of a lighter green than normal, and carrying a yellow overstripe, the colour of the facings. (See the notes on Figure 47 on pages 50–55 for the yellow overstripe.) The yellow is repeated in a broad stripe up the inside of the leg and an even broader band (possibly leather) round the foot of the trews. These have a pinked edge, and show that Sir John wore diced hose under his trews.

In Raeburn's painting, he wears his crimson sash round the waist, unusually since in Highland regiments it was worn over the shoulder. His bonnet is heavily garnished with black feathers and displays no less than three plumes, red, white and yellow. The wearing of a sporran with trews may look surprising, but it was logical, for real 'strap-trews', like the kilt, had no pockets.

Plate 14
Figure 37
The Edinburgh Defence Band was raised in 1781, with a uniform which was presumably designed to show that it was not an army unit (Figure 37). Certainly, a light blue coat with orange lining and facings struck a highly individual note. The hats were perhaps the citizens' own, with the brim tied up in front and behind to make a bicorn, and with a large black feather added to impart a military dash. Cross-belts and muskets were issued by the government to volunteer units, but with considerable reluctance lest the weapons should fall into the wrong hands. Only a year earlier the mob had been masters of London for three days, during the Gordon Riots.

In 1802, the short-lived Peace of Amiens led to the reduction of fencible regiments, but the recurrence of war led to the raising of a new crop of Volunteers.

Plate 14 Figure 38 shows an officer of the Royal Highland Volunteers, formed in 1803.
Figure 38 It is impossible to be wholly precise about the uniform of such bodies because there was evidently a good deal of variation within a unit, and a contemporary drawing or description may reflect a personal whim or the dress worn only by some officers or men. Lawson points out that the cap is interesting as a forerunner of the semi-Highland head-dress adopted later by the 71st on their conversion to light infantry. It signalises a desire to retain something Highland—the diced band round the rim of the bonnet—in what was otherwise the regulation uniform of infantry of the Line.

There was no need for the 42nd Royal Highland Regiment to worry about retaining vestiges of Highland dress, even when the exigencies of a campaign saw them, as in 1784, 'in strong white Ticken trousers', for it was one of the Highland regiments whose dress was never threatened by officialdom. The officer

Plate 15 in Figure 39 is based on another of Dayes's watercolours, about 1790. He is
Figure 39 wearing the Highland version, with no tails, of the cutaway coat seen in Figure 33. Because he wears the half-plaid, his coat fits more snugly over the hips than was possible with the old belted plaid. His white belt was a new feature, for it was in 1789 that the 42nd had abandoned the black sword-belt traditionally worn in Highland regiments for the white belt standard throughout the rest of the army. A waistbelt is concealed by his waistcoat; from it hangs his ornate dirk, with the inset knife and fork, and also, in all probability, his sporran (worn fairly high as was then the fashion) rather than from a narrow sporran-strap round the loins. Note that a pistol is no longer carried as an article of equipment. His bonnet is decorated with a substantial bunch of feathers, but its basic shape is still unmistakable.

Look in contrast at the bonnet worn by an officer of the same regiment about
Plate 16 1808, in Figure 40. His head-dress is such a towering mass of black feathers that
Figure 40 the bonnet is invisible apart from its diced brim. The plume, too is enormous; it is red, a distinction granted to the 42nd in 1795. An Inspection Report of 1790 had complained that 'bonnets are entirely disfigured ... covered with lofty feathers', a charge that could more justly be levelled against the bonnet of this period than that worn by the officer in Figure 39.

The officer of 1808 wears a coat opened at the top to reveal small triangles of the facing colour on the lapels; its cut is generally similar to the coat then worn by all infantry officers. His sash is worn over the left shoulder as was normal, although a plate in *The British Military Library* of 1801 shows officers of the 42nd and 76th wearing a sash round the waist, as well as far less extravagant feather bonnets. The belt plate has become larger and the regimental-pattern sporran more ornate, but on the other hand the plaid is smaller and hangs free at the waist—the purely ornamental 'fly-plaid'.

All Highland regiments, until the mid-nineteenth century, wore red and white diced hose, the 42nd being one of the few whose hose were woven with a very thin black line outlining the checks. This black line tends to appear on all diced hose in contemporary prints or engravings, because it was the simplest way to draw the dicing.

Most of the costly trappings worn by this officer were not likely to appear in the field, and indeed officers of kilted regiments often wore grey trousers in the Peninsula after Wellington gave permission for infantry officers to go mounted on the march. It is therefore hard to know how seriously to take the background of battle in Hamilton Smith's contemporary picture of a grenadier of the 42nd
Plate 15
Figure 41 in 1812, on which Figure 41 is based. The painter was a senior staff officer and claimed that his picture was 'drawn according to the latest regulations', but no regulations have ever reflected what soldiers actually wear on active service. This is probably parade uniform in a romanticized setting.

As a flank company man, this corporal wears wings, and as a grenadier he has a white plume in his bonnet (before long the whole regiment was to wear the red plume or hackle, irrespective of company). It is interesting that the red overstripe seen in Figure 25 still appears in the grenadier's government-pattern tartan. His brown sporran is either fur or hair, perhaps of goat, and his garters are tied in an ornate knot which, like those in Figure 40, may be the rosettes which were worn later in the nineteenth century.

The length of the hose is a curious point. Nearly all eighteenth century paintings and drawings, official or not, show that the hose are gartered where one would expect, a few inches below the knee. At the turn of the century contemporary pictures begin to show the top of the hose coming lower and lower down the leg, with the garter tied at the swell of the calf or even below it. Indeed, they are little more than ankle-hose in Rowlandson's spirited illustrations to *Hungarian & Highland Broad Sword* (1799). But as anyone knows who has worn the kilt—or a pair of shorts with stockings—unless hose are gartered at the top of the calf they will slide inelegantly round the ankles after a dozen paces or two steps in a reel. There was either something peculiarly adhesive about nineteenth-century hose or artists of the period followed one another in believing that a very generous display of bare leg was an essential feature of Highland dress.

Shoulder knots were no longer the badge of rank worn by corporals. In 1803, it had been laid down that, like a sergeant's epaulette, they should be replaced by chevrons formed of a double row of regimental lace. As is the case today, three chevrons were worn by a sergeant, two by a corporal; sergeant-majors and quartermasters had four.

Drummers continued to wear a strikingly distinctive dress, none more so than those of the Household troops. A drummer of the 3rd Foot Guards was painted
Plate 16
Figure 42 by Dayes about 1792, and his picture forms the basis of Figure 42. Instead of a drummer's usual reversed colours, he wears the regimental red coat with its blue

facings, but it is so heavily laced that very little of the red is visible. The lace is not that of the 3rd Guards, nor is it identical to that worn by drummers of the other two regiments of Foot Guards; it is blue with a narrow white edge, and with a row of yellow fleurs de lys running down the centre. Such a lace deserved to be noticed, and so we find it not only on the loops (in three's) and the cuffs but also sewn as a double strip down the chest, down the inside of the arm, and as six double chevrons down the sleeves. As if this were not enough, his rather narrow shoulder-belt and the slings of his drum are painted in the same pattern as the lace.

The red plume in his bearskin cap is a drummer's distinction, but the white-metal front plate and the white cap-cord and tassel were worn by the regiment. Other illustrations of the period show the cord running across the front of the cap, from the base of the plume on the left-hand side down to a point on the right just above the brim, but this drummer appears to have the cord running behind the tall front of his cap. His drum hoops are painted blue, the colour of the facings, with the royal arms in gold.

A drummer of the regiment, painted in 1832, by Drahonet, shows some changes. He wears white epaulettes; the chevrons (perhaps white worsted) are built up and stand proud of the sleeves; the lace appears to consist of blue fleurs de lys on a yellow ground; his plume is white, and his drum-hoops are red. These are changes of detail in what was still, after forty years, a drummer's dress.

Plate 16
Figure 43
·

The private of the regiment, of the early 1790s, in Figure 43 is also based on Dayes's work. He is a 'hat man' i.e. a man of a battalion company. His hat is now to all intents a bicorn with only two points, which resulted in making the folded-up front and rear brims so large that the upright flaps had to be held in position with stays. There were various ways of wearing this ungainly hat; it sometimes appears worn at a slight angle, sometimes nearly parallel to the shoulders. Later, when it became an adjunct to court dress or was worn in the field solely by general officers, it swung through ninety degrees and was worn fore and aft, or very nearly so.

The infantryman's pack was painted with a regimental designation, usually the number or initials; in the case of the Guards, there could be no mistake, as can be seen in the illustration. The pack was supported by two narrow straps over the shoulder, a very tiring way of carrying a load. To reduce the discomfort caused by the straps cutting into the soldier's armpits, a cross-strap over the chest linked the two straps of the pack.

In British nineteenth-century illustrations this cross-strap is shown running under the crossed shoulder-belts, but in a French drawing of 1815, reproduced by Thorburn, it runs over them—see Figure 44, a grenadier of the 3rd Foot Guards in marching order. (Much of the information on what was worn on service by British troops at this period, as opposed to parade dress, comes from French sources.) One suspects that the French artist is right, for it would have

Plate 16
Figure 44

been much simpler to shed the pack if the cross-strap were on top of, and not beneath, the crossed belts.

Thorburn points out that uniform worn on active service was the same for Guards as for Line regiments—short red coat, blue-grey trousers, and shako. Pack, mess-tin and rolled up blanket or great coat were carried on the back; bayonet and ammunition pouch on the cross-belts; the round water-bottle and the cloth haversack were carried on their own separate straps. This soldier wears the new 1812-pattern shako, its white plume indicating that he is a grenadier— the wings on his shoulders could equally have been worn by a light company man. The blue facing of his collar and cuffs was a distinction shared with royal regiments, but his shako plate and belt plate denoted his regiment, as did the fact that his buttons and loops were set on in three's.

Now that trousers were worn as such and not as overalls, they were strapped beneath the sole of the shoe, so gaiters were not worn. Short ankle-gaiters, like the 'spats' worn by Highland regiments, would have increased the infantryman's comfort, but that was an improvement that had to wait for another generation.

The outbreak of war in 1793 had led to the formation of new Highland regiments. Among them was the 79th, raised by Alan Cameron of Erracht who had had an eventful career in his native Lochaber and in America. Unlike other Highland corps, the 79th was not raised by the chief of a clan or the proprietor of large estates but by a private gentleman with a sufficiently independent mind to clothe his men in a new tartan, rather than in the government pattern with or without an overstripe. Although it is certain that the 79th was the only regiment to wear a tartan not based on the government sett, it is less clear exactly how that tartan was evolved by Alan Cameron's mother. She was a MacLean of Drimnin, and the tradition is that she took a yellow stripe from her MacLean tartan and added it to a form of the MacDonald (Alan's grandmother had been a MacDonald) to produce the Cameron of Erracht sett, predominantly dark green, blue and black with bold red and yellow lines. The difficulty in this account lies in the fact that clan tartans as such probably did not exist at the time. The tradition may have been handed on in too precise a form, and could well be true if we substitute 'a sett worn in Morvern and Mull' and 'one worn in and around Lochaber' for MacLean and MacDonald.

Plate 17
Figure 45 Figure 45 shows a private of the 'Seventy Ninth Regiment of Foot or Cameronian Volunteers' as the new unit was officially styled, although Cameron's recruiting poster was correctly headed 'LXXIX Regiment or Cameron Volunteers'. This clerical error persisted, as so often happens, when the name was changed in 1804 to Cameronian Highlanders. Eventually, pressure from the regiment and from the 26th, which had always been known as the Cameronians, was successful and in 1806 the 79th became the Cameron Highlanders. The private's uniform, apart from the unique tartan, was what by now was standard Highland military dress, distinguished by dark green facings. In 1802, and

presumably from its formation, the regiment's lace was white with one yellow and two red stripes running through it. In 1789, as has been noted, the 42nd had adopted a white sword-belt instead of black, and in 1798 other Highland regiments followed suit. Black belts remained a piper's distinction in most regiments.

Plate 17
Figure 46 A lieutenant of the 79th is depicted in Figure 46, which is based on a sketch now in the museum of The Queen's Own Highlanders at Fort George. The artist was Captain Unett of the Royal Artillery, the date perhaps 1811; the regiment had a second battalion in Essex, where the sketch was probably made. Between 1810 and 1814, the 1st 79th was fighting its way in Wellington's army from Busaco to Toulouse, and its uniform on campaign would have been much plainer than this. The officer's double-breasted coat is opened (and held in place across the chest by hooks and eyes) to show the lapels and loops, in contrast to Figure 40.

Captains and subalterns of Highland units had been ordered to stop wearing a second epaulette, but instead a strap on the left shoulder to secure the sash, a regulation that seems to have been frequently ignored. They had also to conform to the regulations over wings with either a grenade on the shoulder strap or—for light company officers—a bugle horn. Lieutenant Ackland, the subject of this sketch, was in the grenadier company, shown by the white plume on his feather bonnet. The latter, which is very high, displays the new fashion for 'fox-tails', a number of longer feathers falling below the brim of the bonnet on the right-hand side and even, on the evidence of this picture, over the forehead as well. After the Peninsular War, the wearing of fox-tails was for a time restricted to officers.

It was in the uniform of this period that three representatives of the 79th—sergeant, piper and private—and of the 42nd and 92nd paraded before the Emperor of Russia at the Elysée when the allies occupied Paris after Waterloo. Sergeant Campbell of the 79th was a man of huge size according to Jameson, and perhaps for that reason was closely inspected by the Emperor, who evidently asked himself the universal question of what a Scotsman wears under his kilt. 'He examined my hose, gaiters, legs' said Campbell, 'and pinched my skin, thinking I wore something under my kilt, and had the curiosity to lift my kilt to the navel, so that he might not be deceived.'

Plate 17
Figure 47 Active service dress for Highland troops is shown in Figure 47, a private of the grenadier company of the 92nd, or Gordon, Highlanders. He wears neither plaid nor sporran, and his bonnet is less exuberant in its display of feathers, though this may be the result of wear and tear. Note the leather peak or eye-shade fitted to the bonnet; this was detachable. The facings of his short coat or jacket are yellow, and the tartan of his kilt is the government pattern with the addition of a yellow overstripe. In addition to his bayonet and ammunition pouch, he carries the standard field-service items—pack, blanket, mess-tin, water-bottle and haversack.

The regiment was formed in 1794 as the 100th, and re-numbered the 92nd three years later; from its foundation it was known as the Gordon Highlanders, although it was not until 1861 that it was officially so titled. It was raised by the Marquis of Huntly, son of the Duke of Gordon whose estates and influence then extended to the West Highlands. The story is well known of how the Duchess helped her son to win recruits by offering a kiss with the usual bounty money of a guinea on enlistment, a story which reflects credit on the recruits as well as on the Duchess, for the lady was in her mid-forties at the time. Perhaps from the new regiment's facing colour, a yellow overstripe was chosen to vary the government sett, creating what became the Gordon tartan in the same way that the Mackenzie came into existence. It was also in 1794 that Sir John Sinclair added a yellow overstripe when he raised his Rothesay and Caithness Fencibles (Figure 36); whether he and the Gordon family hit on this idea independently, or one borrowed from the other, is not known.

It was noted above that in America the value of mobile troops, as scouts and skirmishers, was first realized, even though they were often badly employed. Captain Patrick Ferguson, for instance, of the old 71st Highland Regiment (raised 1775, disbanded 1783), invented and had manufactured a rifle of revolutionary design with which he equipped the light company. With that as a nucleus, he was ordered to raise a corps of riflemen, to be dressed in green. Lord Howe, the Commander in Chief, was far from enthusiastic, and Ferguson got little support in finding and training suitable men. His unit was not used in its intended role, and it was wiped out in North Carolina in 1780. No more was heard, in the British army at least, of his rifle.

Light companies within battalions were only a partial answer to the need, and not nearly as effective as special units equipped and trained for the task. When Sir Thomas Graham raised the 90th Perthshire Volunteers in 1794, the whole body and not just one company was equipped as light infantry. Graham, who had no previous military experience at all, offered a majority in the new unit to Captain Rowland Hill. Both men were to become among the finest of Wellington's generals in the Peninsular War, but the 90th also produced something of equal value—the germ of light infantry training and tactics which Sir John Moore brought to perfection.

The 90th was part of a force sent in 1796 to Portugal, where Major Kenneth Mackenzie was detached to command a composite battalion of all the light companies of the force. When he later took over command of the 90th in Minorca, he applied the principles of training and manoeuvre which he had evolved with his scratch unit, and the result made a deep impression on Moore, who was convinced that the British army badly needed an equivalent to the French *voltigeurs*. When Moore started to train the nucleus of the famous Light Division at Shorncliffe in 1803, Mackenzie was with him, commanding the 52nd Foot, having distinguished himself with his own regiment in Egypt. Ironically, the

90th, where it all began, was not given the official title of Light Infantry until 1815, and never formed part of the Light Division in the Peninsula.

Richard Simkin produced a picture of various ranks of the 90th which he dated 1801, though it probably represents the uniform of a year or two later. **Plate 18** The sergeant in Figure 48 is partly based on this. Since the regiment was planned **Figure 48** from the outset to perform a light infantry role, all ranks wore a short jacket and red waistcoat, with grey breeches and short gaiters. The waistcoats soon became white; the breeches, which evolved into trouser-gaiters and then trousers, earned the 90th the nickname of 'greybreeks', first applied more than a century earlier to the 21st. The sergeant's worsted sash, with a broad central stripe of deep buff, the regiment's facing colour, was of course peculiar to his rank, like the chevrons, but his unusual head-dress was common to all ranks. It resembled a 'Tarleton' or light dragoon cap, consisting of a black leather skull with a metal-bound peak; over the skull from back to front ran a crest of black fur. Just below the front of this crest was a brass bugle-horn badge, the standard light infantry distinction, as was the green plume, This helmet was worn by the 90th for some time after the stove-pipe shako had come into general use.

Plate 18 Figure 49 shows the 1812 or Waterloo shako, the stove-pipe's successor, worn **Figure 49** by a private of the 26th (Cameronian) Regiment. The white-over-red plume in his shako indicates that he is a battalion company man. His leg-wear differs from that of the sergeant in Figure 48 in that he is wearing overalls, over his gaiters; they have not yet become ordinary trousers, as in Figure 44. The shoulder-straps on his coat terminate in a small fringe of white worsted, which was now becoming standard for all infantrymen.

At various times most Highland regiments have had to fight to retain their dress. In 1804, the colonel of the 79th was asked to comment on a proposal then being considered at the Horse Guards (or War Office) to abolish the kilt entirely in favour of trews. Alan Cameron's reaction was vitriolic to 'so painful and degrading an idea ... as to strip us of our native garb ... and *stuff* us into a harlequin tartan pantaloon ... I would sooner see [a Highland soldier] *stuffed* in breeches and abolish the distinction at once.' His letter may have been remembered in 1809 when six Highland regiments were told by the War Office that they were to lose their Highland designation and dress, and instead to be uniformed as regiments of the Line. Five regiments were spared—42nd, 78th, 79th, 92nd and 93rd; the unlucky units were the 71st, 72nd, 73rd, 74th, 75th and 91st. However unpalatable, the decision had a rational basis. The Highlands had been heavily over-recruited despite the population explosion that occurred in the latter part of the eighteenth and early years of the nineteenth centuries, and it had long ceased to be the case that Highland regiments consisted solely of Highlanders. Numbers were made up by recruiting in the Lowlands, in England, and, unofficially, in Ireland but—claimed the War Office—recruits were very averse to wearing the kilt. The kilt was therefore to go, and while they were at it, the authorities decided, in Alan Cameron's prophetic words, to stuff the soldier into breeches and abolish the distinction at once.

Only one of the regiments affected was able to secure some relaxation of the order, the 71st which was to be converted to light infantry. Their objections won the right to retain the word Highland in their title, to continue to have pipers in Highland dress and to retain the bonnet in the shape of a shako. Thus the 71st Highland Light Infantry came into existence. A private of the regiment, about **Plate 18** 1814, is shown in Figure 50. Much of his uniform is standard light infantry **Figure 50** dress, the exception being the strikingly individual head-dress, which has resemblances to that worn earlier by the Royal Highland Volunteers (Figure 38). The usual cocked bonnet when divested of its mass of feathers was called the hummel bonnet, and was sometimes worn on service; hummel is a Scots word meaning unadorned—a hummel stag, for instance, is a beast with no antlers. To turn it into a light infantry cap, it had to be cocked into a new shape or stretched over the shako. In its new guise it kept the peak which had become a detachable feature of the feather bonnet in the field, and of course also retained the diced rim and the two short ribbons at the back. Lawson is the authority for the green toorie, an equivalent of the light infantry's green plume. The usual bugle-horn badge, mounted above the dicing, completed it.

The old 78th Highland Regiment was raised in 1778 by Kenneth Mackenzie, Earl of Seaforth, his recruits in the main being Mackenzies and Macraes from the north and north-west Highlands. On the reduction of many regiments after the American war, it was re-numbered the 72nd. From its foundation until 1809, the regiment wore the belted plaid and kilt of government tartan, with deep yellow facings and bastion loops of regimental lace (white with a green stripe) **Plate 19** on their short red coats. Figure 51, based in part on a Simkin print, shows an **Figure 51** officer at the time of the regiment's formation. His bonnet reveals its shape under the curled bunch of black feathers, a much more elegant head-dress than the fully feathered bonnet of a later period. His sword-belt is black, as was then the rule for Highland regiments—much more sensible, it would seem, than the later white belt. Officers of the 72nd wore silver buttons and lace; surprisingly, Simkin gives officers a single epaulette at this period, instead of the normal two. This may be a mistake, though Simkin worked from detailed descriptions given to him by late nineteenth- and early twentieth-century regimental historians. Note that his inlaid pistol, with its ram's-horn butt, hangs from a waistbelt under his white waistcoat, and not from its own narrow strap over the left shoulder.

In 1793, another Mackenzie regiment was raised, taking the number 78 which had been vacant since the old 78th had become the 72nd in 1786. To differentiate its tartan, the government sett was varied by the addition of two white and one red overstripes. The same pattern, with a difference in the placing of the white stripes, was adopted by the 71st before 1800, probably on the model of the 78th (see p. 40).

Plate 19   A piper of the regiment is shown in Figure 52. Pipers, like bandsmen, were
Figure 52 uniformed in a distinctive fashion, as drummers had always been. In the 78th,
they wore buff jackets, the colour of the regiment's facings, with the additional
distinctions of green wings, and a green plume or hackle in the bonnet. Unlike
Figure 51, the 78th from the start wore a stand-up collar on the coat, and white
belts. It is not clear when pipes themselves began to be decorated with regimental
distinctions. It seems probable that tartan ribbons did not replace tasseled cords
on the drones until well into the nineteenth century, but a tartan cover for the
pipe bag was likely to have been adopted much earlier, particularly when a
regiment had its own pattern, as did the 78th.

Plate 19   A second battalion was raised in 1794 with the additional title of the Ross-
shire Buffs, an allusion to the facings; both battalions were amalgamated two
years later, but once more a second battalion was formed in 1804 and existed as
Plate 19 such until 1817. Figure 53 is a sergeant of the 2nd Battalion, 78th, in 1806.
Figure 53 Sergeants no longer carried the old halberd, but instead a short pike. It was a
weapon, not an ornament (though there appear to be few if any records of a
sergeant's causing much execution with his pike), and as such a cross-piece was
fitted below the head to stop it going too far into an enemy. His sash has the
customary stripe of the facing colour. Observe his garters, which are now
markedly ornamental, with large bows or rosettes and dangling ends.

The Royal North British Dragoons (Scots Greys) was one of George III's
favourite regiments, the reason, it has been said, why it was kept in Britain
throughout the Peninsular War. The regiment more than made up for this by
their achievements at Waterloo. By then their uniform had undergone many
modifications. In 1784, they wore two epaulettes like grenadiers whom they also
resembled in their bearskin caps, but in 1796, when their coats were altered by
having the tails shortened, the epaulettes were replaced by shoulder straps
of the facing colour (blue) and red wings, with regimental lace. The wings
were reinforced with metal plates thick enough to turn a sword cut. Like
all cavalry they were ordered in that year to carry their sword from slings
attached to the waistbelt and not from a shoulder-belt, while their muskets
were exchanged for short carbines—changes which as usual took a long time to
be put into effect.

Plate 20   The trooper or private soldier—they were called both—in Figure 54 is taken
Figure 54 from a watercolour by Hamilton Smith of 1807. His jacket or short cavalry coat
has broad white loops across the chest, decreasing in length from top to bottom,
and also on the coat tails which reveal a blue lining where they are turned back.
The loops on the chest were abolished in 1812; the jacket was then fastened with
hooks and eyes, not buttons, and ornamented with lace on the collar and tails,
and with a band of lace down the front. His red sleeve is visible between the two
stripes on his cuff and his heavy buff gauntlets. The broad white shoulder-belt

carries a black ammunition pouch behind the body, and his sword hangs from slings in accordance with regulations.

At this period, hats were worn as an alternative to the bearskin cap; they were the final bicorn form of the felt hat, worn with the two points parallel to the shoulders. They must have been very difficult to keep on the head, despite strings, when riding at the trot or canter. The black bearskin had a peak, like the shako, with a brass plate in front; after 1815, another small plate bearing the honour 'Waterloo' was added. Originally the fur had only formed the front of the cap, but from about 1800 it had surrounded it, higher in front than at the back. The crown of the cap was only visible from behind; it was red, and carried the device of the white horse of Hanover. Like grenadier caps, the bearskins of the Scots Greys were now decorated with plaited cords and festoons or tassels, white for other ranks and gold for officers. A later watercolour of 1813 by the same artist shows all ranks with gold cap cords and tassels, and an all-white plume; and the cap is secured with a brass link chin-strap.

In 1782, the horse furniture had been changed from blue to red, which certainly appears to be its colour in the earlier of the two watercolours. The second, which is more finished in detail, shows it as blue with a broad gold band round the edge.

Plate 20
Figure 55
There is a picture by Fischer, in the Royal Library, Windsor, of the Royal North British Dragoons in 1814, on which is based the officer in Figure 55. His mount is equipped with a blue saddle cloth edged with a double band of gold. It can be seen that the bearskin is even higher in front, with more ornate cord and tassels, and a more prominent brass plate. The blue facing of his coat is scarcely visible on the heavily laced collar or between the broad gold bands down the front of the coat, but it appears more plainly on his cuffs, below the pointed strips of lace.

A new feature of dress is his overalls, introduced in 1812 to protect the breeches on service. As with the infantry, they were originally loose-fitting blue-grey garments; not until the 1820s, according to the regimental tradition, did overalls replace breeches and were therefore cut to fit more tightly. In Fischer's painting, the overalls are certainly a snug fit, whether or not they are worn over breeches. They had a blue stripe down the outside of the leg which appears in the painting as a double stripe; by 1828, this had been replaced by a wide yellow stripe or, in the case of officers, a stripe of gold lace.

Neither Hamilton Smith nor Fischer depicts any officer or man wearing a plate on his cross-belt, yet Parkyn illustrates a handsome gilt plate of about 1802, with the thistle and rose circled by an inscribed strap, surmounted by a crown and with St Andrew and his cross beneath.

The white plume is of normal height. In the same painting Fischer included officers and men of the 92nd Highlanders (see Figure 56), one of the officers wearing in his feather bonnet so long a red and white plume that it comes right over the top of the bonnet and is secured amongst the foxtails on the right hand side. There appear to be no other contemporary pictures which show such an extravagant plume worn by an officer of a Highland regiment, but curiously Fischer's painting prefigures exactly what happened in the 1830s to the Scots Greys' caps. The leather peak disappeared as the bearskin grew ever larger, while the plume stretched from side to side like a high white crest, until the regiment was ordered to moderate these excesses in 1843.

V: NINETEENTH CENTURY

To our eyes, Waterloo was fought by armies dressed in gaudy uniforms, yet British troops were in many ways more effectively clad for the battlefield than they had been before the Peninsular War, given the fact that command was still exercised on the evidence of what the commander could see. His skirmishers should be unobtrusively dressed but his main force had to be conspicuous, and if possible easily distinguishable from the equally conspicuous enemy. So infantry was still red-coated, though the coat was less encumbering and headgear and netherwear more practical. The item which had seen no improvement, though a crucial one, was footwear. Infantrymen still had to march and fight in crudely made shoes; amidst the mass of treasure and equipment captured at the battle of Vitoria, nothing was more useful for soldiers, who in some cases were barefoot, than a large supply of French shoes. It was not until 1823 that boots first began to be issued to non-kilted regiments, while Highlanders officially wore shoes until 1914, although long before then they had taken to wearing boots on active service. It was not until the middle of the nineteenth century that boots and shoes were made to fit the left or right foot.

The practical lessons of war were soon forgotten after Waterloo, boots being the exception, and uniforms became more ornate in every way. Military fashion no longer modelled itself at least to some degree on civilian style, but increasingly followed its own course in imitation of foreign armies. This was not a new trend—the shako for instance was a French head-dress which in turn had been borrowed from the Austrian army—but it accelerated in the 1820s and 1830s.

Contemporary illustrations can be misleading in that they usually portray the soldier in his finery and not his fatigues; review order made a better picture than marching order. But even if kept for special occasions, uniforms were costly. The system of making stoppages from the soldier's pay for his uniform was diminished and eventually eliminated, although as late as 1858 he still paid for his food, $4\frac{1}{2}$d. in the United Kingdom and $3\frac{1}{2}$d. abroad being docked from his shilling a day pay. The officer, apart from having to buy his various uniforms, had to buy his promotion to a higher rank if a vacancy occurred for which he was qualified—a system that lasted until 1870 because, amongst other reasons, it saved government the cost of paying pensions to retired officers. He also had other calls on his pocket, his share of the band, for instance, since the difference between the pay of a private soldier and that of a trained musician was not met from public funds. Perhaps to keep their expense within bounds, the size of bands was officially limited in 1823 to a sergeant and fourteen musicians. In a Scottish regiment an officer had to pay twice on that account, because pipers, like bandsmen, were regarded as a regimental necessity but a public extravagance.

Plate 21
Figure 56
The elegant officer of the 21st in 1826 in Figure 56 may therefore have had financial worries under his bearskin despite the fact that he would almost certainly have had some private means. His coat or coatee is still waist length in front, but by 1826 officers had been ordered to lengthen the coat tails; the blue facing appears on the collar and cuffs and on the heavily gold-braided front in a final version of the old lapels. As a fusilier, he wears gold wings and gold shoulder-straps embellished with a silver grenade, a device which also adorns his cap. 'Cap' seems an inadequate word for his bearskin, the descendant of the old grenadier and fusilier cap; it was now so lofty that, like the Highlanders' feather bonnet, it had to be kept in place by a chin strap. From 1824, it was not worn overseas except in Canada, and twenty years later it disappeared for a time as a fusilier head-dress, though we will meet it again when the 21st had become the Royal Scots Fusiliers. The bearskin continued to be worn in the interval, however; in 1831, the 3rd Foot Guards were re-named the Scots Fusilier Guards and as such were entitled to the bearskin for all officers and men, and not as previously for the grenadier company alone.

Simkin painted officers of other fusilier regiments of the time, some wearing a cap with the front plate and tasseled cords of the earlier fur cap, and the peak which all headgear acquired during the Napoleonic Wars, while others wear a cap as illustrated; Carman suggests that the grenade cap badge was not introduced until 1831. At this period there was considerable variation in the colour of trousers, from dark blue to light blue-grey, and white trousers were worn in warm weather.

Like other items of dress, shoulder-belt plates were more highly decorated, often gilt for officers, with the device in silver. The plate became markedly regimental in design, with a badge and motto, an emblem of foreign service (the sphinx for Egypt, for instance, the elephant for India) and a selection of one or more battle honours. Scottish regiments of course worked into the design, if it were not already part of their badge, a thistle or St Andrew with his cross, or the star of the Order of the Thistle. There was much less space available on the cap-badge, or bonnet-badge, but the same themes appeared.

Plate 21
Figure 57
A good example can be seen in Figure 57, which is based on a print by Mansion and St Eschauzier of an officer of the 79th, about 1837. He wears a separate bonnet badge and plume holder to accommodate both the Thistle Star and St Andrew's Cross surrounded by a wreath, while his belt-plate, in gilt and silver like the bonnet badge, is ornate. The double lacing on the collar front almost obscures the facing of dark green which is more visible on the cuffs. His

coat is a new pattern, for in 1829 lapels had at last been abolished, leading to a much neater fit across the chest, with a double row of buttons from collar to waist. Buttons and lace had always been gold for the 79th and for most regiments; in 1830, they had been made standard for all, silver being reserved as a militia distinction, so the 'silver lace' regiments like the 71st and 72nd had been obliged to change.

Since 1810, epaulettes had constituted badges of rank. Those of subalterns had a fringe; of captains, a fringe of bullion (thin tubes made from coils of gold wire); those of field officers were larger and carried an embroidered star on top for a major, a crown for a lieutenant-colonel, as well as bullion fringes.

The looped edge of his shoulder plaid is just visible behind the kilt; both of course are of Erracht Cameron tartan. His ornate sporran is regimental pattern though his equally ornate dirk may be his own. Note the black waist-belt, with its gold buckle, just appearing below the laced edge of his coat; as well as holding his kilt in place, it carried the dirk, while the sporran hangs from its own strap. Observe also the two rosettes of dark green silk on the right front of the kilt, something that appears to have been dropped by the 79th although it continued to be worn by some regiments (see notes on Figure 61, page 61).

The original print shows that the dicing of his hose (the mysteriously self-supporting type, despite the elegant garters) stopped at the ankles, which is curious since hose were cut from cloth. It also shows no dicing to the rim of the feather bonnet, which is so unlikely as to be almost certainly wrong. The all-white hackle plume is correct, however; in the 1826 Dress Regulations, it had been confirmed that a hackle-plume of 'red vulture' was to be worn by the 42nd alone, other Highland regiments to wear white. A few years later the difference in colour of plumes between flank and battalion companies was abolished, so white was universal for Highland regiments with the exception of the 42nd.

From this decorative officer in review order we turn to a sergeant of the 92nd in **Plate 21** Figure 58, based on a photograph, now in the Scottish National Portrait Gallery, Figure 58 taken in Edinburgh Castle in 1845 by Hill and Adamson. It also includes a private of the regiment in kilt and feather bonnet, in contrast to the sergeant in undress order. There are several features of interest in his uniform, the first being the fact that he is wearing trews, although the 92nd was one of the Highland regiments which never lost the kilt. Just as in the previous century the 'little kilt' was often worn off-duty and in barracks, trews were now coming to be worn 'off-parade' instead of the kilt.

His white jacket is the descendant of the old sleeved waistcoat worn by all infantrymen, which served as a fatigue coat. It was replaced in 1830 by a red undress jacket, but Highland regiments and the Foot Guards continued to wear the white jacket in drill order. The stand-up collar is open at the neck to reveal his black stock. The stock, of leather or cloth, remained a universal article of dress until the 1860s when it gave way to a small tab of black leather, just visible when the front of the collar was closed. His sash has the regulation stripe of the regimental facing colour; he cannot have worn it much longer, for it was in 1845, the year the photograph was taken, that this stripe was abolished. He wears a rather tall cocked hummel bonnet (i.e. without feathers) with a flattened crown, probably with a badge, although it is hard to make this out in the photograph.

We left the 90th (Perthshire Volunteers) uniformed as light infantry while still infantry of the Line. It had been officially designated as a light infantry regiment for thirty-five years by 1850, the date of the picture by Hayes on which Figure
Plate 22
Figure 59
59 is based, but by that time the light infantry uniform differed only in detail from that worn by other infantrymen. The private's coat displays the 90th's buff facing colour, but his lace is no longer of a regimental pattern since all these had been abolished in 1836, and replaced by plain white. In light infantry units, wings with a fringe of white worsted were worn by all soldiers, not just men of the flank companies. His trouser are dark blue with a red stripe; since 1846, white trousers had been restricted to tropical wear.

His shako is another new pattern, introduced in 1844, and nicknamed the Albert, with a narrow penthouse brim fore and aft. The plume of Peninsular days had now given way to a ball-tuft or pompon, dark green for light infantry. There was a holder for the tuft behind a crown fixed above the shako plate which was inscribed with the usual bugle-horn badge. Light infantry had always used bugles because the normal method of signalling by drumbeat was useless for the dispersed formation in which light troops operated. For the same reason, officers and sergeants of light infantry regiments carried a whistle secured to their belt by a lanyard or chain; rather like the old grenadier's match-case, the whistle became an ornamental feature of light infantry dress.

The private of this illustration is armed with the comparatively recent (1842) percussion musket. It was still a smooth-bore muzzle loader, but the inefficient priming pan and flint had been replaced by a percussion cap, originally invented for sporting guns by the Reverend James Forsyth, a Scots minister who was exasperated by misfires when he went grouse shooting. The infantryman's accoutrements had seen little change in the last forty years, but the cartridge pouch with its overlapping flap top now hung fairly low, on the right buttock. The reason appears to have been to keep the right arm free of the pack when the soldier reached into his pouch. The cross-belts have the usual plate, which carried the only reference to the 90th's Scottish connection—a spray of thistles around a strap inscribed 'Perthshire Light Infantry' which in turn encircled a corded bugle horn and XC.

The 72nd was one of the unlucky six regiments which in 1809 lost their Highland designation and dress, which in its case meant the adoption of a Line regiment's tropical uniform of red jacket, white trousers and round black hat since they were then serving in the Cape. It was the first of the six to succeed in recovering its full Highland status, in December 1823, under the title of the 72nd or Duke of Albany's Own Highlanders, but with the stipulation that the regiment was to wear trews and not the kilt. The tartan they were ordered to adopt was new to the army, a variation of Royal Stewart in what was known as the Prince Charles Edward sett, thought to have been that worn by the Prince when he held court at Holyrood after capturing Edinburgh. The wheel had certainly turned full circle since the Forty Five.

Plate 22
Figure 60
The officer in Figure 60 is drawn from a print published in 1854 by Ackermann. His striking uniform was not in fact a wholly new departure because it resembled that already worn by mounted field officers of kilted Highland regiments, although he has a much deeper fringe to his 'scar' or cross-plaid which is secured at the shoulder with an elaborate brooch. It almost conceals his sash, of which only the knot and fringe on the right side is visible. He wears the regulation single epaulette; in 1855, the year after Ackermann's print was published, this remaining epaulette was abolished. His feather bonnet with its foxtails is the usual pattern, but it may be noted that the white plume curves in to the top of the bonnet. The trews are of what had become the normal style, tartan trousers, no longer cut on the bias for a close fit as had been the case a century earlier.

Plate 22
Figure 61
There is a charming portrait, about 1852, of Sergeant Rennie of the 93rd in walking-out dress, which forms the basis of Figure 61. The sergeant's stripe has disappeared from the sash, which is not secured by the shoulder-strap, despite an earlier regulation to this effect. Wings had been worn, since 1822, by all companies in the regiment, not just the two flank companies. Through the fold of his plaid one can see the handle of his bayonet, hanging from the shoulder-belt; the wearing of a side-arm was a feature of walking-out dress. The badger sporran has always been favoured by the 93rd, and so too the long-tailed silk rosettes on the kilt (compare Figure 57). These have continued to be worn by the 93rd (Argyll and Sutherland Highlanders) and by the 42nd (Black Watch). The rosette was always a decorative finish to a functional ribbon, as with garters or the gorget ribbons, and so it has been conjectured that these ribbons may once have served to secure the front fold of the kilt, as a kilt pin does.

Unlike those of the officer in Figure 57, his hose are diced throughout, and not just to the ankle. His feather bonnet has a diced rim of a pattern unique to the regiment of red and white only, without green squares at the intersections of the dicing. His tartan is the government pattern. Nowadays, under the name of the Sutherland tartan, it is pleated so as to emphasize the dark green in the pattern, rather than the dark blue as in the Black Watch kilt. The unknown painter of Sergeant Rennie's portrait gives his tartan a paler green than in another painting of almost the same date, on which Figure 62 is based.

Plate 23
Figure 62
This depicts a colour sergeant of the 93rd in 1854, in marching order which is why he wears spats, unlike the previous figure. Spats (from the old spatterdashes—see page 25) were a formalised version of the short gaiters worn in

the Peninsula, as in Figure 47, and became normal wear with the kilt. The rank of colour sergeant had been introduced to the army in 1813, and at this period the rank badge consisted of a single chevron beneath crossed swords, which were surmounted by a small union flag and crown. His lofty feather bonnet is protected by an oilskin cover, something which also appears in contemporary paintings of the 92nd (1833) and the 79th (1853), and very odd it looks. Note that the six tassels on his badger sporran are secured in brass sockets or 'bells'; and that, while the tails of his garter ribbons hang nearly to the ankle, the knot is plain, unlike those of Sergeant Rennie or of the next figure, who appears in the same contemporary watercolour, by Poate.

Plate 23
Figure 63

Figure 63 is a bandsman of the 93rd. Since most of the cost of the band was borne by the officers of a regiment, the uniform of bandsmen had never been wholly covered by Dress Regulations, although a general pattern emerged which was then regulated. In 1830, for instance, an order was issued confirming the practice of dressing bandsmen in white but, as far as a number of Highland regiments are concerned, the most striking feature of band uniform was the tartan.

From its earliest days, the 42nd appear to have dressed the bandsmen in a red tartan, in sharp contrast to the dark government pattern. It became known as the Music Pattern, and was adopted by other regiments. There is some doubt (as usual) about its exact appearance in the mid-eighteenth century, but it is thought to have been a form of the Royal Stewart. That is certainly what Poate painted in his watercolour a century later, although the green of the sett is as strongly emphasized as the red and the yellow. With a white jacket instead of a red, and a kilt of a different tartan, the bandsman was markedly differentiated from the rank and file.

His red plume was a usual band distinction, as were the red wings to his jacket, and the red piping on collar, shoulder-straps and cuffs, all of which were the regimental facing colour—yellow in the case of the 93rd. Like a piper, our bandsman carries a broadsword from a black leather shoulder-belt and, as a final distinction, his white hair sporran with black tassels differs from the pattern worn by rank and file.

A number of changes in dress and equipment took place in the 1850s, though experience gained in the Crimean War did surprisingly little to introduce improvements in practicality. Soldiers of course always adapt uniform to circumstances as far as possible and photographs taken in the miserable conditions of the 1854–55 winter show a remarkable range of make-shift attempts to combat the cold and the wet. The 79th returned from the Crimea in 1856, when Major Wymer painted a group of all ranks, showing no sign of the recent war in their

Plate 23
Figure 64

dress. The sergeant of Figure 64 is based on this painting, in which the other characters all wear feather bonnets and the kilt, with the exception of a mounted field officer in trews and a cross-plaid.

The glengarry worn by this sergeant was hardly a new head-dress since in essence it was a hummel bonnet pressed into a fore and aft shape, which made it easier to carry flat. It had orginated in the shape of bonnet adopted, or invented, by MacDonnell of Glengarry for his 'tail' or following at the time of George IV's visit to Edinburgh in 1822. A commanding officer of the 79th introduced it to his regiment, and so to the army, in 1840. In 1851, the glengarry was officially authorised for kilted regiments (it was already being worn by pipers) and by 1870 it had been sanctioned as an undress cap for all infantry regiments. For Highland units, it was to retain the diced rim, and the two black ribbons at the back, of the feather bonnet, but the 79th preferred a plain black rim or border. The glengarry, incidentally, is the only head-dress still to carry the black cockade which the army started to wear in the early eighteenth century.

The same commanding officer altered the dicing of the regiment's hose from the customary red and white to red and green. Green was probably chosen as the 79th's facing colour, changed to blue in 1873 when the regiment became a royal one, as the Queen's Own Cameron Highlanders. The alteration in the dicing of hose was later adopted by the 42nd and 92nd, but as a pattern of red and black.

The sergeant in Figure 64 also demonstrates the new style of turning the top of the hose over the garter, a surprisingly belated innovation which of course disposed of the knot or rosette; instead of long tails, only a short garter flash was now visible. He is in drill order, and so wears the standard white jacket; his brown hair sporran, with its five tassels, is the regimental pattern of the period. His accoutrements are of a new pattern, however, with a single shoulder-belt instead of the old cross-belts, and a waistbelt from which hangs his bayonet. In marching order, his equipment would now consist of a pack with blanket or greatcoat strapped behind it, instead of rolled up on top; the mess tin was perched on top of the pack. He would carry his black ammunition pouch slung below the waistbelt at his back.

The small pouch attached to the sergeant's shoulder-belt carried his supply of percussion caps. The smooth-bore musket had at last been replaced by the Enfield rifle; it was still a muzzle loader, but the Prussian 'needle gun' was soon to demonstrate the inadequacy of such a firearm. Snider's method of converting existing Enfield rifles into breech loaders was adopted in 1865, and once the conversion was completed, all new rifles were produced as breech loaders.

In 1856, the same year that Major Wymer painted the group of officers and men of the 79th, a series of photographs was taken, at Queen Victoria's suggestion, by Cundall and Howlett of 'Crimean Heroes'. One of the sitters was Piper Muir

Plate 24
Figure 65

of the 42nd, the subject of Figure 65. Normally only pioneers and, in certain regiments, pipe majors were allowed to sport a beard, but the rule was relaxed in the Crimea and most contemporary pictures show an array of majestic beards. Piper Muir is no exception.

He is wearing a double-breasted doublet. In 1855, infantry were issued with a tunic coat to replace the old short coat, but the tunic was too long to wear with the kilt and sporran so the doublet was introduced for Highland regiments. In effect, it was the old jacket with four 'skirts' or flaps added to it, and at this period had two rows of diamond-shaped buttons running down the front, with similar buttons on the cuffs and pockets. It had a very short life, for within two years it was replaced by a single-breasted doublet with round buttons, which remained the standard coat for Highland regiments and, after 1881, Lowland also until the abolition of full dress. The diamond-shaped buttons still survive in some forms of civilian Highland dress.

The most interesting thing about Piper Muir's doublet is the fact that it is made from Black Watch tartan, cut on the bias, in contrast to his kilt and cross-plaid which are Royal Stewart. Simkin, who worked with detailed information supplied by the regiment about 1900, painted a piper uniformed like this, though wearing the old short jacket, which he dated as 1852. A tartan doublet was also worn by pipers of the 91st, in the so-called Campbell tartan authorised for the regiment (see the comments on Figure 67, on page 97).

Our piper wears the usual black leather sword-belt over his shoulder, and a waistbelt carrying his dirk, which was also a piper's distinction. The original photograph shows that his pipes carried a pipe banner embroidered with XLII and a badge or device, no doubt his company commander's, but indecipherable; hence the pipe ribbons in the illustration. It became the custom for pipers to wear the glengarry, although in the 1860s the 92nd's pipers wore a flat bonnet or 'balmoral'; but the pipers of the 42nd continued to wear the feather bonnet with the red hackle.

The 92nd and 91st, both Highland regiments, had been refused permission to have pipers in 1852, even though the Lowland 25th and 26th retained their pipers, albeit at the expense of the officers. It was not until 1854, after years of pressure, that the muddled position was to some extent clarified with permission, for Highland regiments only, to carry a pipe major and five pipers on the establishment, any additional ones to be paid for by the regiment, and not until 1918 that all Scottish regiments had an establishment for a pipe major and six pipers.

Plate 24
Figure 66
The glengarry was not the only alternative head-dress to the feather bonnet; a type of forage cap can be seen in Figure 66, taken from a photograph, reproduced by Thorburn, of the 92nd at Stirling in 1861. The cap is an adaptation of the peaked cap worn by various armies in the mid-nineteenth century, the diced band and the red toorie striking a Highland note. As always, there were variations; a photograph taken in the Crimea of a group of officers of the 42nd shows a strip of tartan round the cap instead of dicing. One would imagine that the forage cap was usually worn in undress, but in this photograph it is worn in the same order of dress as the feather bonnet.

2. Lancer, 1643

1. Highland Bowman, 1640

Plate 1

5. Officer of
   Montrose's force, 1644

4. Pikeman, 1644

3. Covenanting officer, 1644

Plate 2

8. Musketeer, 25th Foot, 1689

7. Officer, 1st Foot, 1684

6. Piper, 1st Foot, 1683

Plate 3

9. Sergeant, Foot Guards, 1679   10. Musketeer, Foot Guards, 1686

Plate 4

13. Officer,
    21st Foot, 1690

12. Piper, 21st Foot, 1688

11. Drummer, 21st Foot, 1678

Plate 5

14. Officer, Royal Scots Dragoons, 1680

15. Grenadier, Royal Scots Dragoons, 1687

16. Grenadier, 26th Foot, 1700

Plate 6

18: Trooper, Royal North British Dragoons, 1720

19. Private, 3rd Foot Guards, 1740

17. Private, 1st Foot, 1720

Plate 7

22. Private, 26th Foot, 1742

21. Corporal, 43rd (42nd) Foot, 1742

20. Private, 21st Foot, 1742

Plate 8

23. Jacobite soldier, 1746

24. Grenadier, 1st Foot, 1746

Plate 9

26. Sergeant,
    3rd Foot Guards, 1770

27. Hugh Montgomerie,
    Earl of Eglinton;
    old 77th Foot

25. Grenadier, 42nd Foot, 1751

Plate 10

29. Light Company Officer,
25th Foot, 1770

30. Grenadier, 25th Foot, 1770

28. Piper, 25th Foot, 1770

Plate 11

32. Private, 1st Battalion, old 73rd Foot, 1785

31. Officer, 2nd Battalion, old 73rd Foot, 1780

Plate 12

34. Corporal, Light Company
1st Foot, 1810

35. Officer, 1st Foot, 1815

33. Officer, 1st Foot, c.1790

Plate 13

37. Edinburgh Defence Band,
1782

38. Officer, Royal Highland
Volunteers, 1804

36. Sir John Sinclair, Rothesay & Caithness Fencibles, 1795

Plate 14

40. Officer,
    42nd Foot, 1808

41. Corporal, Grenadier
    Company, 42nd Foot,
    1812

39. Officer, 42nd Foot, 1790

Plate 15

44. Grenadier, 3rd Foot Guards, 1815

43. Private, 3rd Foot Guards, 1792

42. Drummer, 3rd Foot Guards, 1792

Plate 16

46. Officer, 79th Foot, 1813

47. Grenadier, 92nd Foot, 1815

45. Private, 79th Foot, 1793

Plate 17

49. Private, 26th Foot, 1812

50. Private, 71st Foot, 1814

48. Sergeant, 90th Foot, 1803

Plate 18

52. Piper, 78th Foot, 1793

53. Sergeant, 2nd Battalion, 78th Foot, 1806

51. Officer, 78th (72nd) Foot, 1780

Plate 19

54. Trooper, Royal North British Dragoons, 1807

55. Officer, Royal North British Dragoons, 1814

Plate 20

58. Sergeant,
    92nd Foot, 1845

57. Officer, 79th Foot, 1837

56. Officer, 21st Foot, 1826

Plate 21

60. Officer,
    72nd Foot, 1854

61. Sergeant, 93rd Foot, 1852

59. Private, 90th Foot, 1850

Plate 22

62. Colour Sergeant, 93rd Foot, 1854

63. Bandsman, 93rd Foot, 1854

64. Sergeant, 79th Foot, 1856

Plate 23

66. Officer, 92nd Foot, 1861

67. Drummer,
91st Foot, 1875

65. Piper, 42nd Foot, 1856

Plate 24

70. Bandsman, 74th Foot, 1880

69. Officer, 78th Foot, 1865

68. Private, 78th Foot, 1865

Plate 25

71. Private, 72nd Foot, 1879

72. Sergeant, 2nd Dragoons (Royal Scots Greys), 1881

Plate 26

75. Private, Highland Light Infantry, 1895

74. Sergeant, Royal Scots Fusiliers, 1895

73. Private, Cameronians (Scottish Rifles), 1885

Plate 27

77. Private, Queen's Own
Cameron Highlanders, 1910

78. Officer, Royal Scots, 1913

76. Officer, Gordon Highlanders, 1901

Plate 28

81. Piper, Seaforth Highlanders, 1916

80. Sergeant, Seaforth Highlanders, 1915

79. Private, King's Own Scottish Borderers, 1914

Plate 29

83. Officer, Queen's Own
Cameron Highlanders, 1938

84. Infantryman, 1939

82. Officer, Gordon Highlanders, 1936

Plate 30

87. Private, Gordon Highlanders, 1944

86. Drum Major,
Queen's Own Cameron
Highlanders, 1944

85. Private, Black Watch, 1943

Plate 31

90. Officer, Queen's Own Highlanders, 1985

89. Infantryman, 1980

88. Colour Sergeant, Royal Highland Fusiliers, 1978

Plate 32

With his kilt and plaid of Gordon tartan, the officer in this illustration is wearing the single-breasted doublet, introduced about 1857; there is a trim of white piping on the skirts or flaps, the pockets, and down the front, while the yellow regimental facing appears on the collar and cuffs. Officers now wore a waistbelt over the doublet carrying the dirk in addition to the usual sword-belt. The officer's dirk belt had been worn under the double-breasted doublet, as was the case earlier (see Figure 57), but was worn over the single-breasted pattern, and in consequence became more ornate. The leather of the belt was faced with gold lace, or with cloth embroidered in gold wire, in thistle pattern, and it was secured with a rectangular buckle-plate of regimental pattern. The broadsword scabbard was by now suspended on short slings, not from a frog on the belt. The sporran had greatly increased in size, the hair front now hanging down as far as the knee, a feature that was to continue until the end of full dress. The dicing of the 92nd hose was now red and black (see above, Figure 64). This officer wears the India Mutiny Medal of 1857–58.

After epaulettes had been abolished in 1855, badges of rank for officers were embroidered on the collar. In 1880, rank badges for all officers were moved to the shoulder-straps, in the shape of one silver star for a lieutenant, two for a captain, a crown for majors, and crown and star for lieutenant-colonels. The old rank of ensign was, briefly, re-named sub-lieutenant before settling down as second lieutenant, but he had to wait until 1902 before acquiring any badge of rank. He was allotted one star which in turn meant two stars for a lieutenant, three for a captain, as is the case today.

Buglers had long since ceased to be the prerogative of light infantry, but in other regiments they continued to be called drummers, and retained many of the distinctions in dress that had always set drummers apart from the rank and file.
Plate 24 Figure 67 represents a drummer, about 1875, of the 91st Argyllshire Highlanders
Figure 67 which in six years time was to be linked with the 93rd Sutherland Highlanders. The 91st had originally been raised in Argyll as the 98th, and was uniformed in Highland dress with government-pattern tartan until it lost its Highland designation in 1809. A new supply of tartan for kilts and plaids had just been received and was turned into trews, but even these were forbidden in 1810 in favour of grey trousers. The regiment did manage to hang on to its pipers for another generation, until they were so unwise as to parade with their pipers in front of the Adjutant General who ordered their immediate abolition. This blow must have helped the campaign, abetted by the Duke of Argyll, for the restoration of the regiment's Highland status. It was finally achieved in 1864 when the War Office ordered that the 91st were to become a 'non-kilted Highland corps' wearing 'trews of the Campbell tartan', presumably as a compliment to the Duke. But the tartan is quite unlike any Campbell tartan of today, and in fact looks like the old grenadiers' tartan of the 42nd, the government sett with a red overstripe.

The 91st had to wait until their amalgamation with the 93rd in 1881 to recover the kilt.

The drummer in the illustration wears trews of this so-called Campbell tartan; his doublet is the standard Highland pattern, with the new-style gauntlet cuffs of the facing colour. It is decorated with what by now was a universal pattern of drummers' lace, white with red crowns, which in 1864 had replaced individual regimental patterns. The doublet, like the tunic worn by non-Highland regiments, was no longer brick-red, the colour of soldiers' coats for more than one hundred and forty years, but scarlet like those worn by officers.

The War Office order of 1864 had specified a 'chaco: blue cloth with diced band and black braid'. It was worn with a chin-strap and carried a cap badge above the peak, with a plume-holder above it. The plume was now a ball-tuft, which Simkin depicts as the old white-over-red pattern, perhaps inaccurately.

For some reason, the same War Office order laid down that 'the white waistcoat with sleeves, issued to other Highland regiments, will not be worn by the 91st **Plate 25** Foot'. It can be seen worn by the groom or orderly of the 78th in Figure 68 **Figure 68** which is based on a painting by Orlando Norie of about 1865. It will be noted that his sporran is even longer than that of the 92nd officer in Figure 66, and that the 78th had retained the traditional red and white dicing for hose. His glengarry carries a diced band, although a piper of the regiment in the original painting has no dicing on his glengarry.

At this period, the soldier's kilt was made of 'hard' tartan, woven from very tightly twisted yarn of coarse wool which produced a hardwearing and almost waterproof cloth, but it had the great disadvantage on the march, in rain and wind, of flicking against the tender skin at the back of the knees until the hard edge could draw blood. Queen Victoria's sharp eye noticed this in 1870, when the Guard of Honour at Ballater was drawn from the 93rd, and as a consequence of her comments a softer tartan was taken into use.

Plate 25 The charger behind this orderly belongs to the field officer of Figure 69, based **Figure 69** on the same painting by Norie. The tartan of his trews and cross-plaid, as of the orderly's kilt, is the regimental or Mackenzie pattern. It is curious that all contemporary pictures of mounted officers of Highland regiments show them wearing the feather bonnet, which must have been a very awkward form of riding hat. The diced forage cap of Figure 66 seems not to have been worn by mounted officers. Norie painted all the officers and men in his group wearing the old 'flap' cuff, and not the new gauntlet style.

Plate 25 Another type of cuff, favoured for the white jackets of bandsmen, is shown in **Figure 70** Figure 70, based on a Simkin print. He is a bandsman of the 74th Highlanders, which had recovered that lost designation in 1845 and with it the right to wear trews, though not the full Highland dress of the regiment's formation in 1787. Permission was given to vary the government tartan by the addition of a single white overstripe, the resulting sett being known as the Lamont tartan. The bandsman, of about 1880, wears trews and cross-plaid of this tartan which was nearly at the end of its issue as an army pattern; the following year, on becoming the 2nd Battalion Highland Light Infantry, the 74th adopted the Mackenzie tartan of the 71st which became the 1st Battalion (see page 101). His collar and cuffs are red, like the piping down the front of his jacket and on his shoulder straps, which was usual for bandsmen, but unlike Figure 63, he is armed only with a dirk and not a broadsword, perhaps because the bandsman was now looked on as even less of a combatant.

By this date, it was only bandsmen of the Highland corps who wore white jackets. Those of other infantry regiments had been ordered in 1873 to adopt scarlet tunics, differentiated from those of the rank and file by the addition of wings on the shoulders. Wings had not been worn by the infantry for a dozen years before then, since the abolition of flank companies in 1859–60.

Home uniform has always been altered on service overseas, from necessity or for comfort. In India, cotton, which was readily available, was cooler than the heavy red coat and could easily be dyed khaki (dust-coloured). It was worn by the 72nd, among other regiments, in India in the Mutiny and during the Afghan War of 1878–80. An interesting photograph of the officers of the regiment, in their dilapidated mess in Kabul in 1879, is reproduced in *Cuidich 'n Righ*. All were wearing trews in what was still (until 1881) the regimental tartan of the Prince Charles Edward Stewart sett; two are huddled into sheepskin or goatskin *poshteens*; one is wearing the doublet, while half a dozen are in khaki jackets, with the new-fangled Sam Browne belt. Head-dress is the undiced glengarry, with the exception of one officer in a sun helmet, with a blanket tied bandolier-fashion over his shoulder. Like several of his fellows, he is wearing puttees, from his ankles to his calves, made from strips of tartan. The blanket must have been a necessity, for it is recorded that on the famous march to Kandahar the temperature ranged from 110 Fahrenheit at noon to freezing point at night.

Plate 26
Figure 71
The photograph corroborates the accuracy of a Simkin print on which is based the private of the 72nd in Figure 71. Puttees (from the Hindi *patti*, a bandage) were a valuable support and protection to the legs, and were presumably improvised from tartan because strips of cotton cloth did not have the same stretch and resilience as wool. Simkin shows the khaki jacket with what look like two bandolier strips sewn on the chest, but the illustration follows the photograph in giving the jacket two breast pockets with slit openings and no flaps. The topi or sun helmet usually carried a badge at the front, but none appears here; the glengarries of the officers in their mess of course bear the regimental badge of the antlered stag's head.

The emergence of Hussars and Lancers, on top of the trend to richer adornment, brought a wide variety of dress to nineteenth-century cavalry, but in contrast to that of many regiments, the uniform of the 2nd Dragoons (Royal Scots Greys) seems restrained. The changes to be seen between Figure 54, of 1807, and the sergeant of the 1880s in Figure 72 are relatively minor. His scarlet jacket is piped with yellow cord up the front and on the blue collar; his heavy gauntlets conceal similar piping on blue cuffs. His blue 'overalls' are, despite their name, his only nether garment, tucked into his butcher boots. The two-inch wide yellow stripe down the leg was a regimental distinction, as of course was the black bearskin cap with its white plume, much more modest in size than the earlier plume. His shoulder-belt carried at his back a black leather ammunition pouch, and from the white waistbelt hung his sword, from slings.

His carbine, carried in a leather bucket behind which was strapped a mess-tin, was a new pattern. In 1874, the Martini-Henry rifle had been issued, with a shorter-barrelled carbine model, as a replacememt for the Snider Enfield; it was to remain the army's personal firearm until the introduction of the Lee-Metford in 1892 when the soldier would at last have a magazine-loaded rifle.

Prussian military fashion had been copied in the British army after Waterloo with the introduction of a high coat-collar, closely fastened at the front. A much more obvious imitation followed Prussia's victory over France in 1870–71 when the shako began to be replaced by a helmet. Fusilier and Highland regiments escaped it (except of course in the form of the old tropical sun helmet), but it disfigured the dress of all other infantry. The helmet assumed various colours—white, green, black, dark blue—with a central spike of brass or white metal, a leather or metal rim on the pointed peak, and a brass 'chain' chin-strap. A large metal plate at the front carried a regimental badge. It can be seen in Figure 73.

In 1881, there was a radical reorganization of the infantry. All Line regiments with a number higher than 25 (with the exception of the 79th) were linked in pairs to form new two-battalion regiments. In this process the 26th Cameronians and the 90th Perthshire Light Infantry were joined to create Scotland's only rifle regiment, the Cameronians (Scottish Rifles), after a preliminary hiccup when for a few months they were the Scotch Rifles. Rifle regiments had for long been uniformed in dark colours or in black, and the new unit followed suit, although with a Scottish twist. The private of 1885, in Figure 73, wears the current spiked helmet, covered in dark green cloth, the colour of his doublet. At the time of the 1881 reforms it had been laid down that Lowland regiments should no longer be uniformed like other infantry but should wear the trews and, as a consequence, the Highland doublet instead of the tunic coat. In the rifle tradition, the doublet was piped with black cord or braid, and the buttons were black also.

The tartan for the trews of all newly-garbed Lowland regiments was ordered to be the government sett. Like the other units affected, the Cameronians decided that a tartan of their own would be preferable and in 1892 won approval to wear the Douglas tartan, appropriately since the regiment had been raised in Douglas country some two hundred years earlier. At the same time the regiment had the sense and good taste to get rid of their helmets and reverted to the pattern of shako they had worn in the 1870s.

As a rifleman, the private's equipment is of black leather; his rifle is the Martini-Henry.

Because of their number, the 21st was not linked with any other regiment when it became the Royal Scots Fusiliers in 1881. Like the 25th, which that year became the King's Own Borderers, the 21st had always maintained strong links with its native Scotland but unlike other Lowland regiments saw no need to proclaim this by adopting trews. They protested strongly against the imposition of tartan but were over-ruled, and they too appeared in the government tartan

Plate 27
Figure 74 (the Scots Guards were successful in declining the trews). Figure 74 is a sergeant of the Royal Scots Fusiliers of 1895, in the comparatively new uniform. His black leather leggings or gaiters are an innovation for wear with trews.

His doublet carries the blue facings of a royal regiment. Facings had been systematised in 1881, with Scottish regiments wearing yellow, Irish green and English and Welsh white. Yellow facings had for long been associated with Scottish regiments, though by no means exclusively, but those who had worn buff were unhappy at the change. The new rule did not affect royal regiments; paradoxically the Cameronians which as the 26th had always worn yellow, had to change to dark green on their conversion to a rifle regiment. Our sergeant carries the usual fusilier grenade badges on his collar and as a cap badge. The cap was a new pattern, somewhat lower in the crown, made of black racoon or bearskin. There had been changes in the rule governing the wearing of a white plume, which had appeared on the old bearskin and as a ball-tuft and then a tassel on the later shako. The plume was to be worn again by the Royal Scots Fusiliers from the early 1900s, on the right of the bearskin.

The subject of the photograph on which this illustration is based wears a medal. One cannot tell what it is, but since the regiment was engaged in 1885 in Burma, the India General Service Medal with the Burma clasp seems appropriate.

The Highland Light Infantry was created in 1881 by the linking of the 71st and 74th. In such cases, it was generally the tartan of the senior regiment which was adopted, and so the 74th abandoned their Lamont tartan (see Figure 70) for the Mackenzie of the 71st. The rule of seniority and tartan was not, or could not, always be applied. The 72nd and 91st, in trews, and the 75th which had lost Highland dress entirely, adopted the kilt in the tartan of the junior regiment when they were linked with the 78th, 93rd and 92nd respectively to form the Seaforth, Argyll and Sutherland, and Gordon Highlanders.

Plate 27
Figure 75 A private of the Highland Light Infantry in 1895 is the subject of Figure 75, in trews of Mackenzie tartan, and wearing the 1869 pattern shako, the final version of this head-dress before its supersession by the helmet which the Highland Light Infantry succeeded in avoiding. The shako, which retained the diced band worn by the 71st, was made of smooth blue cloth, so dark as to be almost black, although examples exist in dark green like those of other light infantry units; a dark green ball-tuft was worn above the shako-plate. The tuft was removable, so that the shako could be fitted with an oilskin cover in bad weather.

A new type of equipment, the Slade-Wallace, had been issued in 1885, and is shown in this illustration. Its principle was that weight should be carried on a waistbelt supported by braces, with a separate diagonal strap over the shoulder carrying a haversack on the left hip and with a water-bottle on the right slung from its own narrow strap. Two substantial ammunition pouches were attached to the front of the waistbelt, and a rolled blanket, with mess-tin above it, could be secured on the back. A valise or pack could be carried on the braces at shoulder level.

The private's rifle is the Lee-Enfield, which replaced the Lee-Metford in 1895 and looked very similar. With various modifications it was used by the army in both world wars; it was robust enough to stand up to the usual knocks of active service and in the hands of a trained soldier it was capable of sustained and accurate rapid fire.

Boer marksmanship ensured that khaki drill and khaki serge became universal service dress for the army rather than an expedient for particular campaigns. In non-kilted units, trews gave way to drab trousers and long puttees in South Africa, and Highland regiments found it necessary to camouflage the tartan of the kilt by wearing a khaki apron of cotton or ticking. The officer of the Gordon

Plate 28 Highlanders in Figure 76 is wearing one, with a khaki drill tunic. The illustration
Figure 76 is based on a painting by Simkin, who has included on the sun helmet the white hackle worn by all Highland units save the Black Watch. A patch of Gordon tartan is also worn on the helmet.

He is shown with a variation of the Sam Browne belt which carried a leather revolver holster as well as his broadsword. The information or photograph supplied to Simkin clearly related to a period before the regiment had seen much action, for officers soon learned—as they were to do in 1914—that obvious distinctions in dress or equipment made them too inviting a target; the sword was abandoned, and a rifle often carried instead. Spats were still worn, and with brown shoes, although officers soon reverted to black, which other ranks continued to wear. Well fitting spats are in fact comfortable to wear on the march, although a button-hook is required to do them up, but it took World War One to bring the realization that ankle puttees and boots form the ideal footwear for kilted soldiers.

'Service Dress' was officially introduced in 1902 though full dress and undress uniform was still worn as appropriate. For Lowland regiments, the last included a double-breasted dark blue frock coat; Highland officers wore as undress a white shell jacket similar to the long-sleeved white waistcoat which had been worn for

so long by the men. White was still worn in hot weather in India in preference
Plate 28 to the khaki which had originated there, as can be seen in Figure 77, a Cameron
Figure 77 Highlander about 1910.

His sun helmet is a different pattern to that of Figure 71; it gave more shade
for the eyes and, it was hoped, more comfort for the wearer. The white drill tunic
had detachable buttons and badges, so that it could be laundered and kept smart
by the *dhobi wallah*. Shorts were worn in India by this date—the Highland Light
Infantry sensibly converted old trews into tartan shorts—but the kilt was worn
even in hot weather in Highland regiments. It had the advantage of warding off
chills in the belly, a disabling complaint in the tropics, and the corresponding disadvantage of taking a long time to dry after being soaked in sweat on the march.

His sporran is the regimental pattern. Sporrans form a wide field of study,
since every kilted regiment has had a variety of styles for officers and men, with
a different pattern for pipers and sometimes for NCOs. The shape and colour
of the sporran itself, the colour and number of the tassels and their bells, the
pattern of the top and its ornamented rim, and of course the regimental sporran
badge, are capable of very many variations. The sporran of the nineteenth and
twentieth centuries is a far cry from the utilitarian leather purse in which it
originated, and reformers have been quick to recognize the fact; in the early
1920s, its abolition was actively considered. The Highland Brigade has always
been fortunate in having a very independent-minded officer in command of one
or more of its battalions at such moments, and with the help of King George V
the threat was averted.

The nineteenth century may truly be said to have come to an end with World
War One, and it is appropriate therefore to end this chapter with an illustration
of full dress at the end of its life in Line regiments, since there was no reprieve
for it after 1914; amongst other reasons, its cost for a young officer was prohibitive.
Plate 28 Figure 78 represents an officer of the Royal Scots in 1913. As the 1st of Foot,
Figure 78 the regiment did not have to link with any other in 1881 but, like all Lowland
regiments, underwent a complete transformation of uniform. Tunic and red-
striped trousers gave way to doublet and trews of government or Black Watch
tartan, although the spiked helmet continued to be worn, as in Figure 73 but
covered in blue and not green cloth.

In 1901, the Royal Scots were authorised to change their tartan to the Hunting
Stewart, which they still wear, and two years later, in company with what was
now the King's Own Scottish Borderers, were able to shed their inappropriate
helmets for the Kilmarnock bonnet. This was in essence the old hummel bonnet
cocked to form a rather large flat top set at a slight tilt on the broad diced rim.
Strictly speaking, it was not a hummel or unadorned bonnet since it carried as
a plume a blackcock's lyre-shaped tail feathers. Kilmarnock had been the centre
of a bonnet-making industry for a long time, and other patterns had earlier been
called Kilmarnocks, though the name is now reserved for the bonnets worn by
these two regiments.

Our officer wears a shoulder-belt which carries his sword on slings; until 1903, the sword had hung from the waistbelt. He still wears the latter, in the same way that officers of Highland regiments wore a dirk belt, though he has no dirk. The waistbelt buckle, the shoulder-belt plate and the bonnet badge were all of course of regimental pattern. For the Royal Scots, the collar badge was a gold-embroidered thistle. The shoulder-straps on the doublet were now of plaited gold cord on which silver badges of rank were worn. In service dress, as opposed to full dress, rank badges were worn on the cuffs where they officially remained until 1920. In that year, the wartime practice of wearing stars and crown on the shoulder-straps was formally approved.

The major in our illustration wears the Boer War medals (two, since Queen Victoria died in January 1901), the Queen's South Africa Medal and the King's South Africa Medal 1901–1902.

VI: TWENTIETH CENTURY

The British Expeditionary Force went to France in August 1914 wearing the service dress which had been standard since 1902 but with new-style equipment of webbing, not leather. Apart from its material, the principal difference in appearance from the old Slade-Wallace lay in its ten fifteen-round ammunition pouches, six of which were on the waistbelt with two more on each of the braces running from the belt under the shoulder-straps. These one hundred and fifty .303 rounds were held in disposable five-round clips or chargers, two of which loaded the Lee-Enfield's magazine.

This equipment is worn by the private of the King's Own Scottish Borderers in Figure 79. The knee-length puttees, as noted above, had been worn over the trouser legs in the Boer War, a reversion to the long gaiters of the eighteenth century. The surprising aspect of his dress is perhaps the glengarry, the service dress alternative to the Kilmarnock bonnet, but it was worn in the field by all Scottish regiments in the early months of the war. It was found unsuitable, not least in the conditions of trench warfare, and in 1915 a new head-dress was issued, the so-called balmoral or, in official parlance, the Bonnet TOS (Tam o' Shanter).

As can be seen in Figure 80, based on a photograph of men of the Seaforth Highlanders in 1915, the balmoral began as a badly made, poorly shaped flat pancake. The material was thin khaki cloth (though other colours were also tried), whereas the old blue bonnet on which it was modelled had been made of tightly woven woollen yarn, partly felted, so that it was almost waterproof. The new issue was highly unpopular and was soon replaced by a properly made bonnet, with a khaki toorie. It will be noted that the first issue had a couple of khaki ribbons at the back, perhaps to compensate for its inadequacies.

The sergeant is carrying an additional bandolier slung round the neck; these were flimsy affairs made of cloth, to meet the need for extra ammunition in the attack and in the consolidation phase after it. They had the twin defects of cutting into the shoulder and flopping about on the chest and midriff.

The kilt apron had now become a kilt cover, going all the way round, though still usually known by its old name. As in the Peninsular War, the sporran was not worn in the field, and a useful innovation to replace it was the provision of

Plate 29
Figure 79

Plate 29
Figure 80

a pocket at the front of the apron. For kilted regiments, the front of the serge tunic was cut away to allow for the sporran, but in fact many Highland soldiers, particularly in the Territorials and New Army, were issued with the same straight-cut tunics as other infantry. Like other infantry, too, Highlanders at last had proper boots, but with hose-tops and ankle puttees. The illustration follows the photograph in showing puttees wound from the outside of the ankle to the inside, which is unusual.

It is not clear when hose-tops replaced full hose. Their advantage of course is that they are worn with socks, which can be washed, darned or worn out and thrown away long before the hose-top needs replacement. Hose-tops can be worn with spats as easily as with ankle puttees, and since diced hose were expensive, such an obvious measure of economy was probably adopted soon after spats became regulation dress.

The Bonnet TOS in its improved form was a more practical cap than the glengarry, but it was no protection against shrapnel. The first steel helmets appeared in 1916, and thereafter bonnets were only worn out of the line. Figure **Plate 29** 81 is in part drawn from a photograph, reproduced in the history of the Queen's **Figure 81** Own Highlanders, of a piper of the Seaforths leading the 7th Battalion out of action at the Somme, and underlines the role that pipers have always played on the battlefield. Like the other men in the original, he wears the new steel helmet, and no kilt apron, probably because the latter, always of flimsy material, had simply fallen to pieces.

There is controversy about the wisdom of retaining the kilt in the appalling conditions of trench warfare, although there appears to be little doubt about its powerful effect on morale. At least one veteran has declared that the kilt was far better than trousers in the trenches, since one could hold it up when traversing really deep mud and still have a dry nether garment; there appear to be few diaries or letters complaining that it was impractical.

Between the wars, service dress was normal parade uniform. Figure 82, an officer **Plate 30** of the Gordon Highlanders in 1936, is based on a photograph of a Guard of **Figure 82** Honour at Ballater. His uniform is essentially similar to the service dress worn twenty-five years earlier. With the Sam Browne belt, the sword was carried on a leather frog, not from slings as in full dress. The standard frog was not ideal for the Highland broadsword, which led (as usual) to regimental variations and sometimes to the replacement of the basket hilt with a cross hilt when the sword was carried in service dress. The officer in this case has retained the basket hilt to his broadsword—which the War Office for a long time persisted in erroneously calling a claymore.

Plate 30 A walking stick was often carried by officers in service dress, as in Figure 83, **Figure 83** a field officer of the Cameron Highlanders, about 1938. The cross-plaid and trews had been worn by mounted officers of Highland regiments (see Figure 69); the equivalent in service dress was tartan breeches, reinforced inside the knee with a patch of soft black leather, and either back riding boots or knee-length puttees, dark blue in this case. The regimental adjutant had by now been added to the roster of field officers, and the establishment of majors had long been increased from the single major who assisted the early eighteenth-century colonel and lieutenant-colonel in their duties of command and administration. This major's medal ribbons denote the Military Cross and the three World War One service medals, irreverently known as Pip, Squeak and Wilfred.

Some changes in the long history of British uniform have originated at regimental level, with subsequent official sanction, while others have been laid down from on high. In the late 1930s, the revolutionary step was taken of creating a new service dress from scratch with the object of designing an outfit that would be efficient, comfortable and durable. As can be seen in Figure 84, smartness came low down on the list of desirable qualities; smartness at the expense of serviceability had led to too many mistakes in the past.

Plate 30
Figure 84

The private's equipment resembled that worn in World War One, but the ten ammunition pouches were replaced by two larger ones designed to carry magazines for the army's new light machine gun, the Bren, carried by each of the three sections of an infantry platoon. The use of gas had led to the carrying of a box respirator by 1918, and the threat was taken even more seriously before World War Two. An improved respirator was carried on the chest and an entirely new article, the anti-gas cape, designed as a protection against mustard gas, was rolled up on top of the small pack. The latter was an enlarged haversack and was carried on the back intead of hanging at the side from the waistbelt.

Trousers, well supplied with pockets, were tucked into webbing ankle gaiters, which were less effective than ankle puttees would have been. But the principal defect in battle-dress, as the new uniform was called, was the short blouse which had buttons at the back to secure it to the trousers. The buttons always gave way, leaving the soldier with a chilly gap in the small of the back. The battle-dress blouse, however, made a splendid kilt jacket, which was not at all what the authorities had in mind.

For battle-dress was planned to be the universal service uniform for all arms, corps and regiments of the army, and differentiation was frowned on—although Scottish regiments had won the right to wear the balmoral with battle-dress instead of the new fore and aft cap which afflicted all other soldiers. The kilt was the most glaring example of differentiation, and its prohibition not long after the outbreak of war generated much ill feeling. Despite this, thanks to another of those independent-minded commanding officers, the 1st Battalion Cameron Highlanders went to France wearing the kilt and were still so dressed in the retreat to Dunkirk in 1940. The Camerons were thus the last regiment to have worn the kilt in battle, having also been one of the last four regiments (in 1885, in the Sudan) to have worn the scarlet doublet in the face of the enemy.

Battle-dress gave way to khaki drill shirt and shorts in the Middle East, to bush shirt and slacks of drab green in the Far East, but both 'worn with a difference'. The private of the Black Watch in 1943, of Figure 85, has discarded the steel helmet he wore at Alamein in favour of his balmoral for the advance across the desert. His regimental badge is worn, on a patch of tartan, on the balmoral, with the famous red hackle. It was incidentally in the Western Desert in 1939 and 1940 that the army found that sun helmets were unnecessary after a century and more of believing that strong sun was fatal to an unhelmeted head.

Regimental 'name plates' of brass were worn on the shoulder-straps of the shirt, removed when it was necessary to conceal a regiment's identity. Insignia were also worn on the sleeve of the shirt or battle-dress blouse—in this case, the emblem of the Highland Division with a patch of Black Watch tartan below it. The policy of non-differentiation had foundered on the fact that soldiers, like anybody else, want to identify with their comrades in a unit of their own, and the first prerequisite is to make that unit identifiable.

With drill shorts went khaki hose-tops, ankle puttees and boots; a red garter flash was usually worn, purely as an ornament.

Figure 86 shows the Drum Major of the 2nd Battalion Queen's Own Cameron Highlanders, based on a photograph of the pipes and drums playing before an enthralled Italian crowd in San Marino after its capture from the Germans in 1944. Even if the kilt were proscribed on the battlefield, Highland regiments contrived to include in their baggage enough kilts, sporrans and glengarries to equip at least their pipes and drums, and missed no opportunity of some music when out of the line. The Drum Major's staff was as important to the turn-out, even if he lacked his full peacetime panoply, as the drums themselves.

He wears the regulation webbing belt, bleached white with sunshine and scrubbing. The usual patch of regimental tartan was worn immediately below the divisional emblem, in this case the red eagle of the 4th Indian Division. As countless hikers and Scouts in Scotland know, shirt-sleeves and the kilt form an exceedingly comfortable dress.

In contrast, the soldier of Figure 87, in North-West Europe in 1944, wears battle-dress. He is not in the line or on duty, so is not wearing his equipment or steel helmet, which by that date was a different pattern, the brim being narrower, and turning slightly down rather than out. His balmoral indicates that his regiment is Scottish, his cap badge and sleeve patch that it is the Gordon Highlanders. The balmoral was worn tilted to a variety of angles at the wearer's whim (until the C.S.M. put his foot down). 'Scrugged down' over the right ear was the preference of the man in the photograph on which this illustration is based. At that time, the bonnet was not cluttered up internally with wire stiffeners which appears to be the general practice today.

The most far-reaching reorganization of the infantry since 1881 began in 1948 with the reduction of all regiments to a single battalion, save the Parachute

Regiment and the four regiments of Gurkhas which now came on the British establishment. Between 1958 and 1970, the resulting sixty-four regiments were reduced to twenty-eight (of which six have more than one battalion) by disbandment or amalgamation. In the former category came the Cameronians, disbanded in 1968 after close on two hundred and eighty years of distinguished service; in the latter, the Royal Highland Fusiliers was formed by amalgamating the Royal Scots Fusiliers and the Highland Light Infantry, while the Seaforth Highlanders and the Queen's Own Cameron Highlanders were joined to create the Queen's Own Highlanders.

Plate 32
Figure 88
Figure 88 represents a colour sergeant of the Royal Highland Fusiliers (Princess Margaret's Own Glasgow and Ayrshire Regiment) wearing No. 2 Dress as laid down in current Dress Regulations. This is the equivalent of the inter-war service dress, with an open collar worn with shirt and tie. His waistbelt buckle carries the grenade which has always been the fusilier badge, as do his collar and cap badge. His Mackenzie trews are of course the tartan worn by the Highland Light Infantry, which also wore white ankle spats. Pipers of the regiment wear kilt and plaid of the red Erskine tartan which had been adopted by pipers of the Royal Scots Fusiliers in 1928 to mark the two hundred and fiftieth anniversary of that regiment's formation. The colour sergeant carries a warrant officer's silver-knobbed stick, and wears the General Service Medal, which was instituted in 1962 and continues to be awarded for service in action.

Battle-dress went on being worn after World War Two but experience in Korea and then of action in areas as far apart as Borneo and Northern Ireland has led to entirely new dress and equipment. A loose hip-length combat smock was introduced in 1970, made of DPM or 'disruptive pattern material', with trousers of the same or a drab material. Initially boots and ankle puttees were worn with this outfit, since replaced by a flexible calf-length boot. The infantryman in
Plate 32
Figure 89
Figure 89 on duty in Northern Ireland could belong to any Scottish regiment unless one looked at his bonnet badge or the detachable cloth badge worn on the shoulder-strap. His equipment is olive green, with metal buckles and strap ends painted to match, or black. Ammunition pouches are attached to, and below, the waistbelt, giving freer movement to the arm than did the old pouches which rose above the belt. Weight-carrying is now on the rucksack principle, with the load distributed between the back and the small of the waist.

The Lee-Enfield rifle had a long run, and it is unlikely that its successors will be in service for anything like the same period, given the pace of weapon development. The army wanted a self-loading rifle, i.e. one in which the chamber was automatically reloaded, using the force of the waste gases resulting from the discharge of the previous round, and in 1954 got its first SLR, the Belgian FN.

Under Dress Regulations, a regiment has a series of numbered orders of dress, many of them relatively minor variations, ranging from fatigues to ceremonial. The modern soldier spends very little of his extremely active life on ceremonial duties and is much more commonly uniformed in working dress or combat gear. But he can 'put on the style' when the occasion demands, and it seems appropriate to close this selection of Scottish military dress with an example of No. 1 Dress.

Plate 32
Figure 90 Figure 90 is an officer of the Queen's Own Highlanders, which has retained both tartans of its component regiments. The kilt of officers and men is the Seaforth's Mackenzie tartan, while pipers, drummers and bandsmen wear Cameron of Erracht; when trews are worn for barrack duties, the position is reversed. Thus every member of the regiment wears the two tartans in different orders of dress. Badges on the head-dress, belt plate, dirk-belt buckle and sporran blend elements from the badges of the two old regiments.

The officer wears a royal blue hackle in his glengarry, a fairly recent distinction inherited from the Camerons to whom it had been awarded by King George VI in France and worn by them in 1940. The hackle then went into abeyance until 1951, when it was officially sanctioned by the War Office, and is worn by the successor regiment in both balmoral and glengarry.

Another item of his dress calls for comment, the *sgian dubh*, or black knife, stuck into the right hose-top with its silver-mounted black handle protruding. It was not part of old Highland dress, though references exist to a sleeve knife or armpit knife, presumably a small knife concealed on the person; it seems to have come into being in the early nineteenth century as part of the rush of blood to the head over Highland dress and trappings. It was first worn in civilian dress and, like the glengarry, was later unofficially taken into military use, no doubt at first for pipers. The first official reference to the *sgian dubh* is in the 1860s, so officers of Highland regiments must have been wearing it by then, although there is a curious lack of pictorial reference until near the end of the century.

This officer's predecessor in any Highland regiment two centuries ago would not have recognized the *sgian dubh*, and would have been surprised at the spats and at the absence of the full plaid, but he would not have an instant's hesitation in recognizing a Highland soldier. That is a mark of the long thread of continuity which runs through the history of Scottish, and particularly Highland, military dress.

APPENDIX
REGIMENTAL TITLES
AND NUMBERS

Regiments raised in the seventeenth century were first known by the name of the founder, usually a nobleman given a royal commission to do so, and subsequently by the name of its colonel—logically, since the regiment was to some extent his property. Its name accordingly altered when the colonelcy changed hands, or if the colonel was elevated to the peerage. The regiment which eventually became the Royal Scots Fusiliers had five names between 1700 and 1710—Row's, Mordaunt's (twice), De Lalo's and Orrerry's.

Alongside this form of designation, as popular as it was inefficient, a system of numbering was evolved and regularised in William III's reign at a council of general officers in Flanders in 1694. Under this system, a regiment's 'rank' or seniority was defined by its number. This was important because when the funds voted by Parliament for the army were cut at the end of a war, the junior regiments were the first to be disbanded—an early example of 'last in, first out'. It was not until 1753 that the colonel's name ceased to be part of a regiment's title.

Numbering was not without its difficulties, too. The War Office had a tidy mind and so, when a regiment was disbanded, the vacant number was re-allotted to another unit, or a gap in the sequence filled by moving all higher numbered regiments up so many places. These practices particularly affected Highland regiments formed in the second half of the eighteenth century.

The lists that follow do not attempt to give the names of successive colonels; changes in the official titles of regiments make them long enough as it. For the reader's convenience, each regiment is headed by its best known designation of the period between 1881 and 1959.

The Royal Scots Greys

1668–1707	Royal Regiment of Scots Dragoons
1707–1751	Royal Regiment of North British Dragoons
1751–1866	2nd or Royal North British Dragoons
1866–1877	2nd Royal North British Dragoons (Scots Greys)
1877–1920	2nd Dragoons (Royal Scots Greys)

| 1920–1971 | Royal Scots Greys (2nd Dragoons) |
| 1971– | Royal Scots Dragoon Guards (Carabiniers and Greys) |

The Scots Guards

1662–?1686	Regiment of Foot Guards in Scotland
?1686–1712	Scotch Regiment of Foot Guards
1712–1831	Third Regiment of Foot Guards
1831–1877	Scots Fusilier Guards
1877–	Scots Guards

The Royal Scots

1633–1637	Hepburn's Regiment
1637–1653	Le Régiment de Douglas
1653–1688	Earl of Dumbarton's Regiment of Foot
1684/1688–	
1751	Royal Regiment of Foot
1751–1812	1st or Royal Regiment of Foot
1812–1821	1st Regiment of Foot or Royal Scots
1821–1871	1st (The Royal) Regiment of Foot
1871–1881	1st or Royal Scots Regiment
1881	The Lothian Regiment
1881–1920	The Royal Scots (Lothian Regiment)
1920–	The Royal Scots (The Royal Regiment)

The Royal Scots Fusiliers

1678	Earl of Mar's Regiment
?1685	became Fusiliers
1707–1712	Regiment of Scots Fuzileers
1712–175?	Royal North British Fuziliers
1751–1877	21st (Royal North British Fusiliers) Regiment of Foot
1877–1881	21st Royal Scots Fusiliers
1881–1959	The Royal Scots Fusiliers
1959–	(with H.L.I.) Royal Highland Fusiliers (Princess Margaret's Own Glasgow & Ayrshire Regiment)

The King's Own Scottish Borderers

1689–1751	Earl of Leven's on formation; also The Edinburgh Regiment, with colonel's name.
1751–1782	25th (or Edinburgh) Regiment of Foot
1782–1805	25th (or Sussex) Regiment of Foot
1805–1881	25th (The King's Own Borderers) Regiment of Foot
1881–1887	The King's Own Borderers
1887–	The King's Own Scottish Borderers

The Cameronians (Scottish Rifles)

a)

1689–1751	Earl of Angus's on formation; The Cameronian Regiment, with colonel's name
1751–1782	26th Regiment of Foot
1782–1881	26th (or Cameronian) Regiment of Foot
1881	The Cameronians (Scotch Rifles)
1881–1968	(with 90th) The Cameronians (Scottish Rifles)
1968	Disbanded

b)

1794–1815	90th (Perthshire Volunteer) Regiment of Foot
1815–1881	90th (Perthshire Volunteers) (Light Infantry)
1881	(with 26th) 2nd Battalion The Cameronians (Scottish Rifles)

The Black Watch

a)

1739–1749	The Highland Regiment or 43rd Regiment of Foot
1749–1758	re-numbered 42nd Highland Regiment of Foot
1758–1861	42nd Royal Highland Regiment of Foot
1861–1881	42nd Royal Highland Regiment of Foot (The Black Watch)
1881–1934	(with 73rd) The Black Watch (Royal Highlanders)
1934–	The Black Watch (Royal Highland Regiment)

b)

1786–1809	73rd (Highland) Regiment of Foot (formed in 1780 as 2nd Battalion of 42nd)
1809–1862	73rd Regiment of Foot
1862–1881	73rd (Perthshire) Regiment
1881	(with 42nd) 2nd Battalion The Black Watch (Royal Highlanders)

The Highland Light Infantry

a)

1777–1786	73rd Highland Regiment or Lord MacLeod's Highlanders
1786–1808	re-numbered 71st (Highland) Regiment of Foot
1808–1809	71st (Glasgow, Highland) Regiment of Foot
1809–1810	71st (Glasgow, Highland Light Infantry) Regiment
1810–1881	71st (Highland) Regiment, (Light Infantry)
1881–1923	(with 74th) The Highland Light Infantry
1923–1958	The Highland Light Infantry (City of Glasgow Regiment)
1958	(with Royal Scots Fusiliers) Royal Highland Fusiliers (Princess Margaret's Own Glasgow & Ayrshire Regiment)

b)

1787–1816	74th (Highland) Regiment of Foot

1816–1845	74th Regiment of Foot
1845–1881	74th (Highlanders) Regiment of Foot
1881	(with 71st) 2nd Battalion the Highland Light Infantry

The Seaforth Highlanders

a)

1778–1786	78th Regiment of (Highland) Foot
1786–1809	re-numbered 72nd (Highland) Regiment of Foot
1809–1823	72nd Regiment of Foot
1823–1881	72nd (The Duke of Albany's Own Highlanders) Regiment of Foot
1881–1961	(with 78th) The Seaforth Highlanders (Ross-shire Buffs, The Duke of Albany's)
1961–	(with Queen's Own Cameron Highlanders) The Queen's Own Highlanders (Seaforth and Camerons)

b)

1793–1795	78th (Highland) Regiment of Foot
1795–1881	78th (Highland) Regiment of Foot or Ross-shire Buffs
1881	(with 72nd) 2nd Battalion, The Seaforth Highlanders (Ross-shire Buffs, The Duke of Albany's)

The Queen's Own Cameron Highlanders

1793–1804	79th Regiment of Foot or Cameronian Volunteers
1804–1806	79th Regiment of Foot or Cameronian Highlanders
1806–1873	79th Regiment of Foot or Cameron Highlanders
1873–1881	79th Queen's Own Cameron Highlanders
1881–1961	The Queen's Own Cameron Highlanders
1961–	(with Seaforth Highlanders) The Queen's Own Highlanders (Seaforth and Camerons)

The Argyll and Sutherland Highlanders

a)

1794–1798	98th Argyllshire Highlanders Regiment of Foot
1798–1809	re-numbered 91st Argyllshire Highlanders Regiment of Foot
1809–1820	91st Regiment of Foot
1820–1863	91st (or Argyllshire) Regiment of Foot
1863–1872	91st (Argyllshire) Highlanders
1872–1881	91st (Princess Louise's Argyllshire) Highlanders
1881	(with 93rd) Princess Louise's (Sutherland and Argyll Highlanders)
1881–1920	Princess Louise's (Argyll and Sutherland Highlanders)
1920–	The Argyll and Sutherland Highlanders (Princess Louise's)

b)

| 1800–1861 | 93rd (Highland) Regiment of Foot |

| 1861–1881 | 93rd (Sutherland Highlanders) Regiment of Foot |
| 1881– | (with 91st) 2nd Battalion, Princess Louise's (Sutherland and Argyll Highlanders) |

The Gordon Highlanders
a)

1797–1798	100th (or Gordon Highland) Regiment of Foot
1798–1861	re-numbered 92nd (Highland) Regiment of Foot
1861–1881	92nd (Gordon Highlanders) Regiment of Foot
1881–	(with 75th) 2nd Battalion, The Gordon Highlanders

b)

1787–1809	75th (Highland) Regiment of Foot
1809–1881	75th Regiment of Foot
1881–	(with 92nd) 1st Battalion, The Gordon Highlanders

Finally one must add a Scottish regiment which crossed the Border in the 1881 amalgamations, the 99th.

1824–1832	99th Regiment of Foot
1832–1874	99th (Lanarkshire) Regiment of Foot
1874–1881	99th (The Duke of Edinburgh's) Regiment of Foot
1881	(with 62nd) 2nd Battalion, The Duke of Edinburgh's (Wiltshire Regiment)

BIBLIOGRAPHY OF
SOURCES CONSULTED

The place of publication is London unless otherwise stated.

Uniform

Barthorp, M. *British Infantry Uniforms since 1660* Poole, 1982
  British Cavalry Uniforms since 1660 Poole, 1984
Carman, W. Y. *British Military Uniforms* 1957
  Richard Simkin's Uniforms of the British Army Exeter, 1985
Haswell Miller, A. E. and Dawney, N. P. *Military Drawings and Paintings in the Royal Collection* 2 vols, 1966, 1970
Lawson, C. C. P. *A History of the Uniforms of the British Army* 5 vols, 1940–67
Money-Barnes, Major R. & Kennedy, C. *The Uniform and History of the Scottish Regiments* 1960
Myatt, F. *The British Infantry 1660–1945* Poole, 1983
Scobie, Maj. I. H. McK. *The Scottish Regiments of the British Army* Edinburgh, 1942
Society for Army Historical Research: *Journal* passim.
Strachan, H. *British Military Uniforms 1768–96* 1975
Thorburn, W. A. *Uniforms of the Scottish Infantry 1740–1900* Edinburgh, 1970
Wilkinson-Latham, R. *Scottish Military Uniforms* Newton Abbot, 1975

Badges

Bloomer, W. H. & K. D. *Scottish Regimental Badges 1793–1971* 1982
Parkyn, Maj. H. G. *Shoulder Belt Plates and Buttons* Aldershot, 1956
Wilkinson, F. *Badges of the British Army 1820–1960* 5th edn, 1982

Weapons

Cormack, A. J. R. *The History and Development of Small Arms* Windsor, 1982
Rogers, Maj. H. C. B. *Weapons of the British Soldier* 1960

Tartans

Adams, F. *The Clans, Septs and Regiments of the Scottish Highlands* Edinburgh, 7th edn, 1965

Munro, R. W. *Highland Clans and Tartans* 1977

Scarlett, J. D. *The Tartans of the Scottish Clans* 1975

Stewart, D. C. *The Setts of the Scottish Tartans* Edinburgh, 1950

Sutton, A. and Carr, R. *Tartans: Their Art and History* 1984

Regiments

Balfour, C. B., *The Scots Guards* Glasgow, 1919

Balfour-Paul, J. *History of the Royal Company of Archers* Edinburgh, 1875

Blacklock, M. *The Royal Scots Greys* 1971

Buchan, J. *History of the Royal Scots Fusiliers* Edinburgh, 1925

Cannon, R. *Historical Records of the British Army: 42nd Foot* 1845; *1st Foot* 1847; *72nd Foot* 1848; *21st Foot* 1849; *74th Foot* 1850; *73rd Foot* 1851; *92nd Foot* 1851; *71st Foot* 1852; *2nd Dragoons* 1857

Carter, T. *Historical Records of the 26th or Cameronian Regiment* 1867

Fairrie, Lieut.-Col. A. *Cuidich'n Righ: A History of the Queen's Own Highlanders (Seaforth and Camerons)* Inverness, 1983

Higgins, R. T., *Records of the King's Own Borderers or Old Edinburgh Regiment* Edinburgh, 1872

Jameson, Capt. R. *Historical Records of the 79th Foot or Cameron Highlanders* Edinburgh, 1863

Keltie, J. S. *A History of the Scottish Highlands, Highland Clans and Highland Regiments* 1877

McCance, H. H. *Records of the Royal Scots* Edinburgh, 1913

Stewart, Col. D. *Sketches of the Character and Present State of the Highlands of Scotland* Edinburgh, 1822

Sym, Col. J. *The Seaforth Highlanders 1788–1954* 1962

General

Childs, J. *The Army of Charles II* 1976
The Army, James II and the Glorious Revolution Manchester, 1980

de Fonblanque, E. B. *Administration and Organization in the British Army* 1858

Guy, A. J. *Oeconomy and Discipline: Officership and Administration in the British Army 1714–63* Manchester, 1985

Robertson, J. *The Scottish Enlightenment and the Militia Issue* Edinburgh, 1985

Stevenson, D. *Alasdair MacColla and the Highland Problem in the Seventeenth Century* Edinburgh, 1980

Terry, C. S. ed. *Papers Relating to the Army of the Solemn League and Covenant 1643–1647* Edinburgh, 1917

Tomasson, K. and Buist, F. *Battles of the '45* 1962

LIST OF PLATES

Plate 21

56. Officer, 21st Foot, 1826
57. Officer, 79th Foot, 1837
58. Sergeant, 92nd Foot, 1845

Plate 22

59. Private, 90th Foot, 1850
60. Officer, 72nd Foot, 1854
61. Sergeant, 93rd Foot, 1852

Plate 23

62. Colour Sergeant, 93rd Foot, 1854
63. Bandsman, 93rd Foot, 1854
64. Sergeant, 79th Foot, 1856

Plate 24

65. Piper, 42nd Foot, 1856
66. Officer, 92nd Foot, 1861
67. Drummer, 91st Foot, 1875

Plate 25

68. Private, 78th Foot, 1865
69. Officer, 78th Foot, 1865
70. Bandsman, 74th Foot, 1880

Plate 26

71. Private, 72nd Foot, 1879
72. Sergeant, 2nd Dragoons (Royal Scots Greys), 1881

Plate 27

73. Private, Cameronians (Scottish Rifles), 1885
74. Sergeant, Royal Scots Fusiliers, 1895
75. Private, Highland Light Infantry, 1895

Plate 28

76. Officer, Gordon Highlanders, 1901
77. Private, Queen's Own Cameron Highlanders, 1910
78. Officer, Royal Scots, 1913

Plate 29

79. Private, King's Own Scottish Borderers, 1914
80. Sergeant, Seaforth Highlanders, 1915
81. Piper, Seaforth Highlanders, 1916

Plate 30

82. Officer, Gordon Highlanders, 1936
83. Officer, Queen's Own Cameron Highlanders, 1938
84. Infantryman, 1939

Plate 31

85. Private, Black Watch, 1943
86. Drum Major, Queen's Own Cameron Highlanders, 1944
87. Private, Gordon Highlanders, 1944

Plate 32

88. Colour Sergeant, Royal Highland Fusiliers, 1978
89. Infantryman, 1980
90. Officer, Queen's Own Highlanders, 1985

INDEX